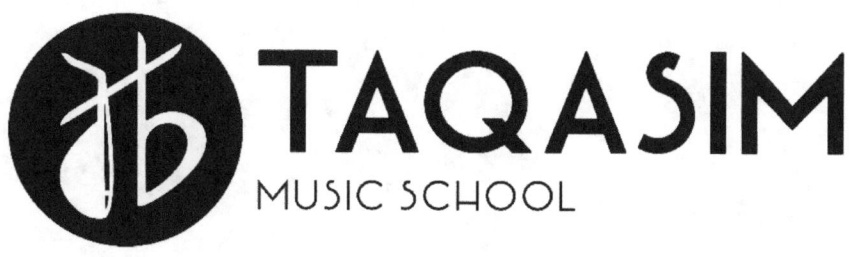

THE MUKHTAR METHOD:

OUD - ADVANCED

By

Ahmed Mukhtar

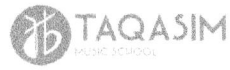

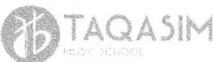

© 2019 Ahmed Mukhtar

ISBN 978-0-244-74418-2

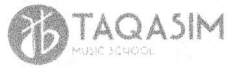

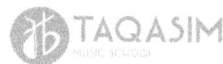

Table of Contents

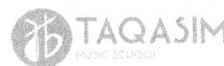

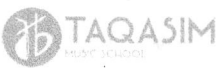

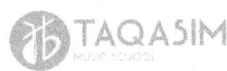

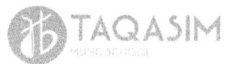

Forward

The composing of a teaching method for any musical instrument is a challenge, but the writing of a method for the Oriental Oud is, by its very nature, a monumental achievement. The Oud carries a prestigious millennial tradition stemming from Ancient Babylon, of a musical system systematically different from the Western model. It is the soul of Oriental philosophy, in the classical sense of the term, and its teaching requires such wisdom that the spirituality contained within can blossom into the limitless sophistications of *Maqam* expressionism. As with classical string instruments such as those of the string quartet, the Oud is fretless, therefore free from the limitations of tonality and open to a universe of modality.

This comprehensive method is progressive and covers all aspects of the Arabian musical system with two levels of theory, and a practical approach in six steps: Beginners; Upper beginners; Intermediate; Upper intermediate; Advanced and Upper advanced.

The method, at all levels, introduces a concept unique to Oriental music, the *rouhiyyah*, by which musicians, through the music they play, reach a state of spiritual enlightenment which is at the core of the Maqamian expression.

During my working life as an Orientalist, I have met with the few illustrious Oud Masters. With them we had endless discussions on method, on interpretation, but it is only with the Maestro Ahmed Mukhtar that I have found a true dedication to the teaching of the instrument. His method applies rigor with a gentle touch. Through his punctilious method Ahmed Mukhtar has adapted the traditional methods to the requirements of Western neophytes and thus contributed to a Western understanding of the Oriental thought.

For these reasons, and many more, I can but only give my sincere and heartfelt congratulations to Maestro Ahmed Mukhtar's excellence not only as a remarkable soloist but also as a dedicated educator in one of its most complex forms which is the art of the Oud.

Richard Dumbrill
December 2018

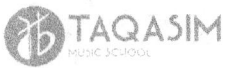

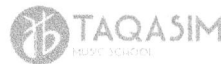

Acknowledgements

The Mukhtar Method curriculum started as a research project as part of my studies at SOAS while earning an MA in Music Performance in 2004. The Beginner level curriculum was further developed in 2009 and used to teach my private oud students as well as those I taught at SOAS. One year later, the Taqasim Music School was established, and the Oud Beginner book was used as the core material for the course. In 2013, the Oud Upper Beginner Book was written and used. Over the years, other books were developed (and continue to be developed) to create the full series. Much time and effort has been spent in the research and development stages of this teaching method.

The completion of this book was made possible by the contributions of many. I would like to offer a heartfelt thank you to:

Mike Smith,
who began to edit the book content from the early stages of development since 2009.

Ahmed Beyh,
for the book cover photography.

Ruba Hillawi,
for contributing to the completion of all books in the series by editing their content, and layout.

Emma Vazquez,
for designing the Taqasim Music School logo.

Seung Hee Ko (Erika),
for designing the book covers for the entire Mukhtar Method series.

Ahmed Mukhtar

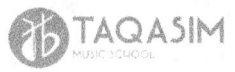

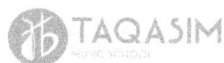

Introduction

The Oud Advanced book has been designed for students who are comfortable playing the Oud using a high level of technique and wish to further advance their playing skills. Students are required to have completed the Upper Intermediate book with a high level of achievement and be able comfortably read music notation without the use of tablatures.

This book will cover multiple techniques of oud playing including a high level of applying ornamentation patterns such as: *qarar* and *jawab*, the use of *trills*. Modulations, secondary *maqamaat* and the use of all three playing positions will also be practiced. These techniques will be practiced and applied while playing a variety of complicated repertoires providing students with a challenging set of skills to improve their playing.

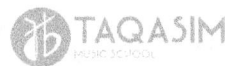

Terminology

Aqid: An Arabic musical term similar to a tetrachord/jins using 5 consecutive notes in a maqam.

Glissando: "Passing all or part of the way from one note to another on the same string." **

Jins (pl. Ajnaas)/Tetrachord: The first 4 and last 4 notes in a scale.

Maqam: A scale used in Arabic music which contains 6 definitive tones and carries a specific mood and spirit.

Micro-Tone (Quarter-Tone): "An interval smaller than a semi-tone."**

Modulation: The smooth transition from one maqam to another related maqam within a given piece of music.

Transposition: The writing or performance of a composition (or scale) at a different pitch from its original (keeping the same intervals).**

Trill: An ornamentation comprised of a rapid alternation of one note and the note above it within a maqam.**

Leading Note: "The 7th degree of a major or minor scale, a semitone below the tonic."**

Taqasim: A term simply defined as "musical improvisation", although far more complex. The main difference is that the performer uses traditional pre-composed musical phrases linking each of those phrases using improvised lines. The phrases used can be played in a variety of ways using different ornamentation.

Tarab: A state of musical ecstasy.

Tone: The unit of measurement used in the tonal system to measure intervals between notes.

Tonic (Settled Note): The first degree of the scale of a maqam. The maqam starts, settles and ends using this note.**

Scale: A group of intervaled notes that ascend or descend in order. This series of notes within a given octave is used to compose any given piece of music.

Secondary Maqam: A maqam that shares its first jins/tetrachord with one of the primary maqamaat.

Sensitive Note: A distinctive note of a scale which allows the listeners to identify/define the maqam being played.

Solfeggio: Method of vocal sight-reading.*

Vibrato: "Vibrated". An undulating, tremulous effect used on stringed instruments and voices to increase the emotional quality of the note."*

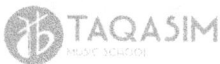

Resources

The following dictionaries have been used as references to define and/or paraphrase some of the above definitions.

* Lovelock, William. *A Student's Dictionary of Music.* G.Bell & Sons, 1979.

** Kennedy, Michael, Tim Rutherford-Johnson, and Joyce Kennedy. *The Oxford Dictionary of Music.* OUP Oxford, 2013.

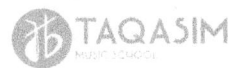

Reading Resources

Below is a list of reliable resources to read for extra information about the history of Arabic music and the Oud.

English Resources

Farmer, Henry George. *A History of Arabian Music to the XIIIth Century*. Luzac, 1929.
The Arabian Influence on Musical Theory. H. Reeves, 1925.

Racy, Ali Jihad. *Making Music in the Arab World : The Culture and Artistry of Ṭarab /*. Cambridge Middle East Studies ; Cambridge ; New York : Cambridge University Press, 2003.

Sawa, George Dimitri. *Music Performance Practice in the Early c Abbasid Era 132-320 AH / 750-932 AD*. 01 edition. Toronto, Ont., Canada: Pontifical Institute of Mediaeval Studies, 1989.

Shiloah, Amnon. *Music in the World of Islam: A Socio-Cultural Study*. Wayne State University Press, 2001.

Touma, H. H. *The Music of the Arabs /*. New expd. ed. Portland, OR : Amadeus Press, 1996.

Arabic Resources

أنور، صبحي رشيد. تاريخ العود. دار علاء الدين، 1999

تاريخ الموسيقى العربية. مؤسسة باڤاريا، 2000.

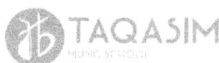

Arabic Musical Forms

Samaa'i

The *samaa'i* is typically made of four sections and a refrain. A section is referred to as a *khanah (khanat pl.)* and the refrain is called *taslim*. A key feature of a *samaa'i* is that each *khanah* is composed using a different *maqam*. The first *khanah* and the *taslim* share a *maqam*, while the 2nd, 3rd and 4th *khanat* are composed using different *maqamat*. The first three *khanat* are written using the *rhythm known as Samaa'i Thaqil*, or 10/8 time, while the fourth is written at an up-beat pace of 3/4 or 6/8 time known as *Samaa'i Darij*.

Longa

The *Longa* is an instrumental form written using a 2/4 time signature and is made of several *khanat*. Each *khanah* followed by a *taslim*. However, that the last *khanah* is usually written in 3/4 time. A *longa* is quite lively and is played at high tempos.

Tahmilah

The *tahmilah* is an instrumental piece played using alternating sections played by an ensemble as well as solo instruments. The parts played by the ensemble are relatively fixed compositions, whereas the solos are mostly improvised, providing plenty of room for individual expression.

Doulab

A *doulab* is a short, instrumental prelude normally performed in unison by an ensemble. Its purpose is to introduce the audience to the maqam that will be played in the coming piece of music. A doulab achieves this by presenting the basic structure and mood of a given *maqam* prior to presenting it elaborately in a coming piece of music and/or song.

Taqasim

Taqasim refers to pieces that are semi-improvised forms and are usually without rhythmic accompaniment. A *maqsoum* (sl.) is meant to demonstrate the structure of a particular *maqam* and its relation to other *maqamaat*. Its performance is a highly skilled art and relies on an intimate knowledge of the structure of the different *maqamaat* and their interrelation. When performing, an artist will follow the general flow of a *maqam*, while emphasizing important tones and using key melodic phrases while modulating to several related *maqamaat*.

Sirto

A *sirto* is similar to the *longa* in that it is usually played in 2/4 or 4/4 time. Some sirtos combine different time signatures such as 2/4 and 7/8 in the same piece.

Free-style Piece

This type of composition has been known in Arabic music since the beginning of the 20th century. It usually contains 2 or 3 movements played in the order of A, B, A, C. In this book the piece titled *Sulaf* is one such example.

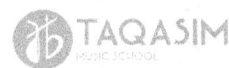

Left Hand Positions (fingers)

There are several positions on the oud. In each position, every string uses all four fingers to cover the entire span of that position.

Position changes are indicated within the tablature lines using the abbreviation "pos....." followed by the position numbers "1", "2" or "3"

The first, second and third positions of the left hand are illustrated here:

1) In the **1ˢᵗ position**, the thumb of the left hand rests on the neck of the oud just below where the neck and the peg box meet. The thumb needs to remain stationary.

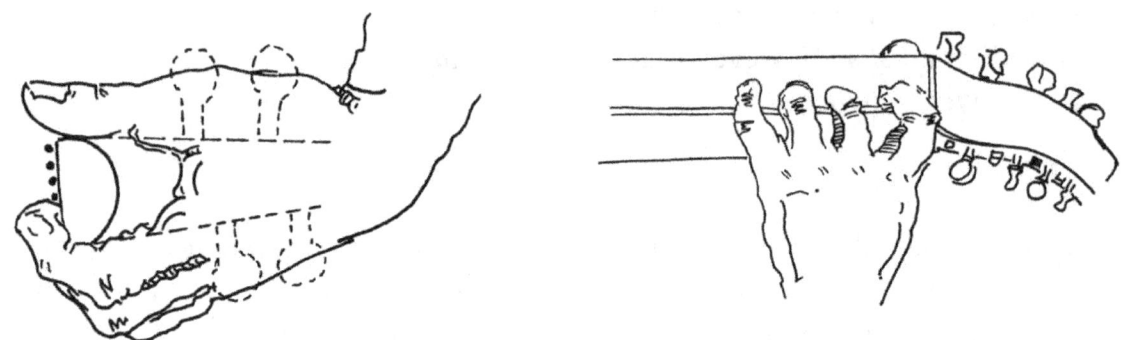

2) In the **2ⁿᵈ position**, the thumb slides approximately half way down the neck of the Oud. The same fingering technique is used.

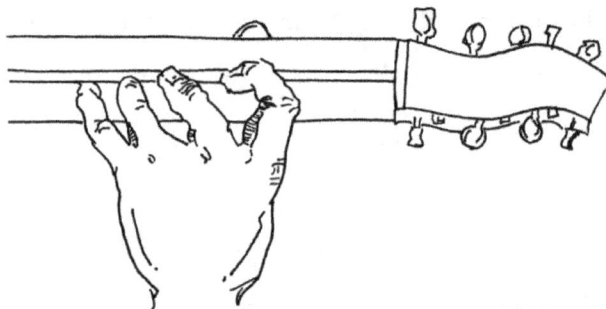

3) In the **3ʳᵈ position**, the thumb slides further down the neck of the Oud resting where the neck meets the body. The same fingering technique is used.

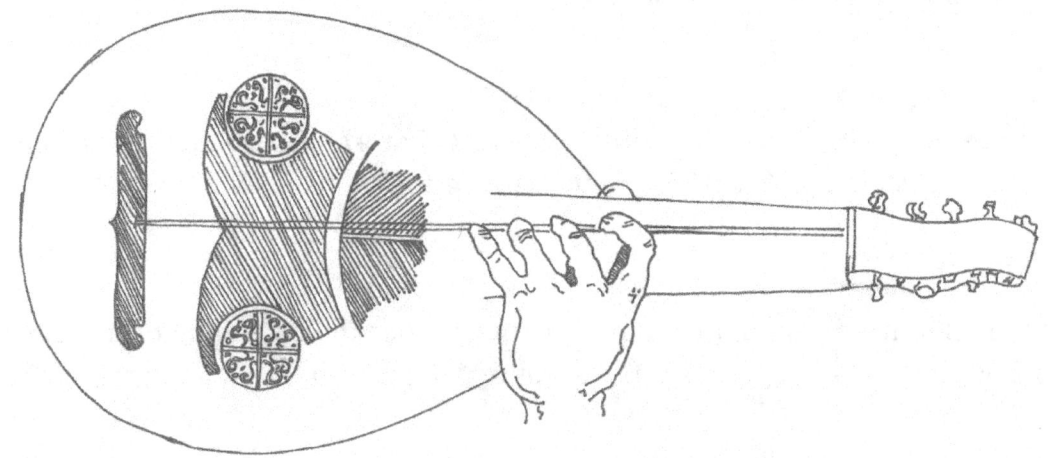

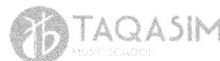

Ornamentation/*Zakhrafah*

Ornamentation – An Overview

The Concise Oxford English Dictionary of Music defines Ornamentation (or Ornaments) as the "embellishments and decorations of a melody as expressed through small notes or special signs."

In Arabic music, the ornamentation, or *zakhrafah*, of a musical score are an essential part of a performance. However, it is not common practice to write out the ornamentation in a musical score. It is usually left up to the musician to add various ornamentations onto a piece. The composer gives the performer creative license to add his/her own interpretation of the music being played. In a sense, the performer is considered to be a second composer. This is why pieces seem to sound different from one performer to the next depending on the ornamentations used.

A musician has a very wide range of ornamentations to choose from. The *zakharif* (pl.) used while playing a piece would depend on both the piece being played as well as the performer's playing skills.

As an ensemble, performers would usually use a set or ornamentative features that have been pre-determined and practiced as a group. As a solo performer, a musician has more freedom in choosing how to present a composition.

This book will explore basic ornamentation techniques with an emphasis of applying them to compositions that have already been studied. By doing so, students will begin to acquire a sense of how and where a variety of ornamentations can be applied well. With time, students will be more confident applying these techniques and skill sets on their own.

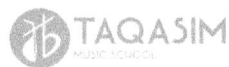

Forms of Ornamentation

Doubled Note: To double a note, an extra strike is added to the single beat that a note usually carries.

Glissando: The movement of the finger up or down one note or a series of notes on a single string. **

Short-tremolo: On the Oud, a short-tremolo is the continuous, rapid down-up *risha* strokes of a string that lasts for a note's short duration. This would usually apply to *noir* notes (quarter-notes), and notes of a shorter duration.

Tremolo: On the oud, a tremolo is the continuous, rapid down-up *risha* strokes of a note that lasts for a note's duration. This would usually apply to *blanche* notes (half-notes), whole notes, and combined notes of a longer duration.

Trill: An ornamentation comprised of a rapid alternation of one note and the note above it within a *maqam*.*

Qarar & Jawab:

- **Qarar**: The low-pitched tone in a lower octave that is paired with and corresponds to its equivalent higher pitched note (*jawab*) in the next/higher octave. For example: a low-pitched Do paired with Do, one octave higher.

- **Jawab**: The higher-pitched tone in a higher octave that is paired with and corresponds to its equivalent lower pitched note (*qarar*) in the lower octave. For example: a high-pitched Do paired with Do, one octave lower.

Vibrato: Italian for "vibrated". In stringed instruments, it is the undulation of a pitch produced by the controlled vibration of the player's finger. ** It is used to increase the emotional quality of a tone.

Resources

* Kennedy, Michael, Tim Rutherford-Johnson, and Joyce Kennedy. *The Oxford Dictionary of Music*. OUP Oxford, 2013.

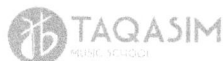

Ornamentation – General Rules of Application

Notes Used

As a general rule, basic ornamentations are added to the notes of a score that last for a longer duration when compared to other notes which form the whole piece. This gives the musician enough time to apply additional techniques without playing out of beat and losing the tempo.

In this book, a focus will be placed on adding ornamentations to:

- Quarter notes →

- Half notes →

- Whole notes → **O**

  and sometimes

- Dotted notes →

Doubling a Note

It is most common to apply this technique on quarter notes. Each quarter note carries the duration of a single beat. A player can add an extra *risha* strike to the given note making sure to remain within the tempo of the piece.

For example:

- 1 risha stroke = 1 beat →

- 2 risha strokes = 1 beat →

Glissando

When playing the oud, the *glissando* is applied by moving the finger from the main note being played to a higher or lower note within the given *maqam* interval located on the same string.

For example, an ascending *glissando* can be applied from Mi to Fa. It can also be applied from Mi to Fa# or to Sol on the same string.

A descending *glissando* can be played from Mi to Mi*b* or from Mi to Re on the same string.

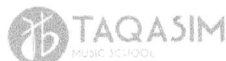

Long and Short Tremolos

Some of the music provided in this book already has a few suggested tremolo ornamentations written into the notation itself. The symbols used to suggest the use of a tremolo are:

- Long tremolo →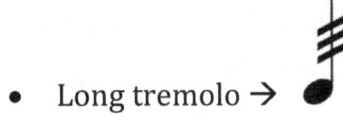

- Short tremolo →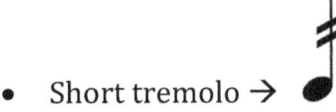

Note: A tremolo lasts for the duration of the note value itself.

The number of lines drawn through a note indicate both the number of strokes in a tremolo as well as their speed.

Using tremolo strokes rather than repeatedly writing out note heads can not only save space when writing on a score but will also result in a piece of music that is easier to read.

For example if notated:

- Three tremolo strokes on a quarter 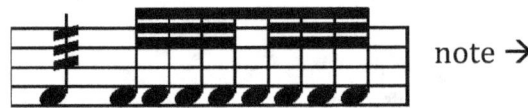 note →

Here, the topmost measure of 3 quarter notes is of equal value as the lowermost measure of three groups of 8 sixteenth notes.

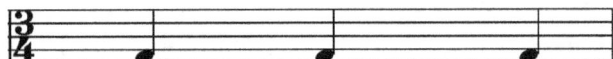

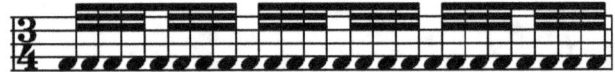

So, playing the topmost measure using tremolos will result in the same auditory experience as playing the bottommost line as written.

Trill

Trills are an essential form of ornamentation in Arabic music. A *trill* is achieved by playing one note of a *maqam* and tapping the next note up. The first note is struck by the *risha,* while the second is only tapped on the finger-board.

A *trill* can be written on the score as seen here →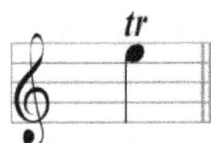

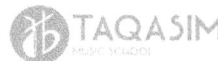

Qarar and Jawab

Playing the same note on two different octaves is a common form of ornamentation in Arabic music. This technique is called *qarar* and *jawab*. As mentioned earlier, *Qarar* refers to the notes of a lower octave/pitch while *jawab* refers to the notes of a higher octave/pitch.

At this stage, play the *qarar* and *jawab* ornamentation with notes that use an open string in the lower (*qarar*) or higher (*jawab*) pitch. Those would include: Do, Re, Fa, Sol and La.

Playing Mi and Si using *qarar* and *jawab* would require using two fingers and no open strings. This technique will be covered at a later stage.

There are several ways in which to apply this technique. The two most basic are:

- Playing each note of *qarar* and *jawab* by striking each of them once

and

- Striking the *qarar* note once and playing *jawab* using a tremolo

Deciding on which of the above techniques to use would depend on the length of the note it is being applied on and whether or not it sounds harmonious with the rest of the piece.

Vibrato

The *vibrato,* or a vibration, can be described as a shake.

To play a *vibrato* on any given note, a player moves his/her finger back and forth on the string by about 2mm higher and lower than the pitch being played. This is usually done to add feeling and emotion to the note and, in turn, the *maqam*, *taqsim* or musical piece.

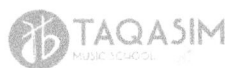

List of Abbreviations

Below is a list of abbreviations that will be used throughout the book. Use these to annotate the ornamentations used on the scores by writing the abbreviations provided below or above the note/s to which the ornamentation applies. If more than one form of ornamentation applies to a single note, write out the abbreviations in the order of which they will be played.

- **Doubling the note →**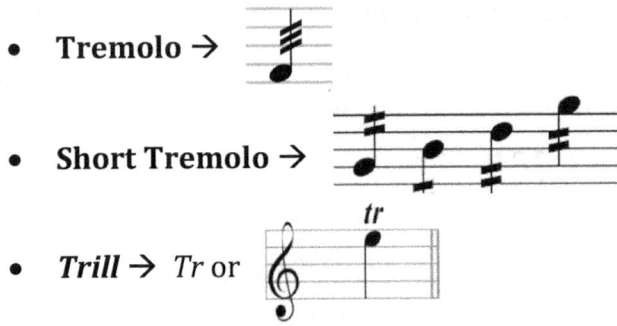

- *Glissando* → Gliss.

- **Tremolo →**

- **Short Tremolo →**

- *Trill* → *Tr* or

- *Qarar & Jawab* → Q

- *Qarar & Jawab* (with Tremolo) → Q and

- *Vibrato*→ Vib.

A single form of ornamentation or several forms can be added to a single note. If more than one form of ornamentation is added then a plus sign (+) will be added in between each abbreviation, if needed, to indicate the use of multiple ornamentative forms.

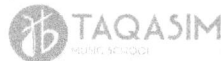

Adding Ornamentation

Since the ornamentation of Arabic music is usually left up to the musician/performer, ornamentations used will be added to the scores, with the help of the teacher, as students progress. This will help with acquiring a better understanding of how ornamentation works.

If you using this book without the help of a teacher, follow the guide provided adding ornamentation to the notes based on the information offered here.

Note: Sometimes, the result of adding too much ornamentation to a piece of music is counterproductive. It is important to keep a balance between playing a note as written and playing a note with the addition of ornamentation. Knowing when to add *zakhrafah* to a piece comes with practice, patience and trial and error. So, feel free to experiment with various possibilities while practicing.

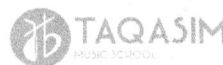

Rhythm/*Iqa'*

A rhythm or *iqa'* is a rhythmic pattern or cycle in Arabian music. It is also called a *darb*, *mizan* or *usul*.

An iqa' is a repeated circular rhythm that can be played using different time signatures. It is estimated that there are over 100 iqa'at (pl.). However, some are more widely used than others.

Rhythm notation:

Notation is used to write out circular rhythmic patterns on a single line. Those notes can be read as follows:

- Dum → heavy beat →

- Tak → light beat →

- Silent →

The word *wazn* is used to refer to the time signature, and the iqa' is the pattern created within a given time signature. Each pattern within a *wazn* is given a special name. For instance, one of the common time signatures used is 8/8. However, there are several *iqa'at*, or circular rhythmic patterns, that are written based on this time signature. Below, are a few examples of different patterns written in 8/8 and 4/4 time:

- *Maqsoum*, written in 8/8 time:

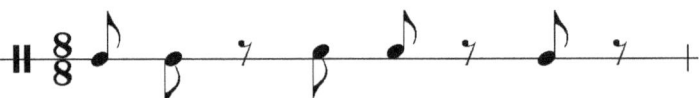

- *Malfouf*, also written in 8/8 time:

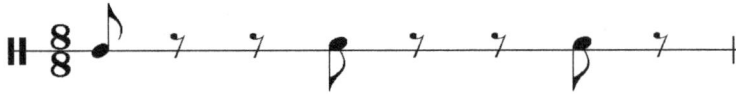

- *Hachaá*, written in 4/4 time:

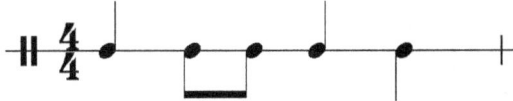

- *Ayoub*, also written in 4/4:

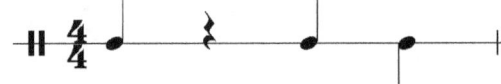

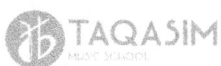

Common Iqa'aat/Rhythms

The following is a list of the most common *iqa'at* used in Arabic music:

Samaa'i Thaqil

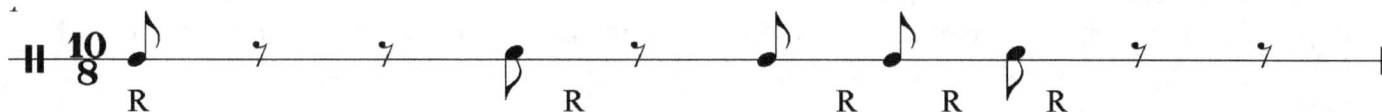

Darij

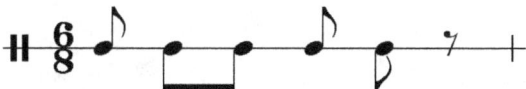

Maqsoum

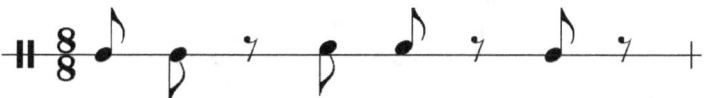

Fox

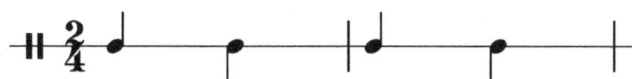

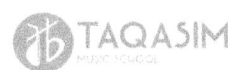

Ajnaas (sl. *Jins*)/Tetrachords

Maqam scales are made up of smaller sets of consecutive notes that have a very recognizable melody and convey a distinctive mood. Such a set is called *jins* (pl. *ajnaas*), meaning "genus" or "kind". In most cases, a *jins* is made up of four consecutive notes. *Ajnaas* are the building blocks of a *maqam* scale. A *maqam* scale has a lower (or first) *jins* and an upper (or second) *jins*. In most cases *maqamaat* are classified into families or branches based on their lower *jins*. The upper *jins* may start on the ending note of the lower *jins,* called *jins mutasil (*connected) or on the note following that, called *jins munfasil* (disconnected). In some cases, the upper and lower *ajnaas* may overlap.

The main *ajnaas* are shown below:

Jins Ajam

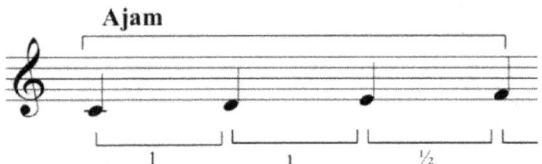

Jins Rast

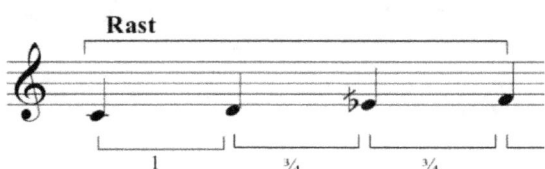

Jins Nahawand

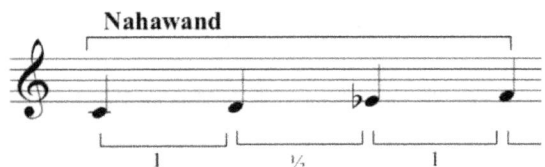

Jins Bayat

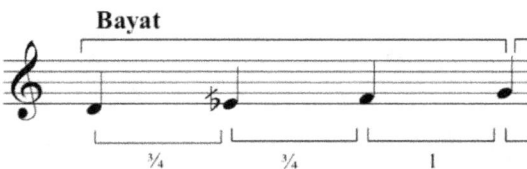

Jins Kurd

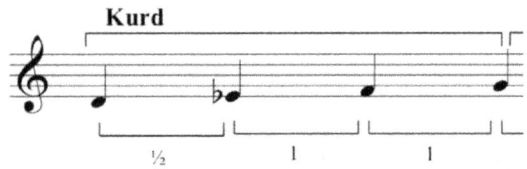

Jins Saba

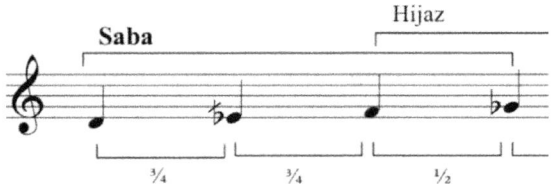

Jins Hijaz

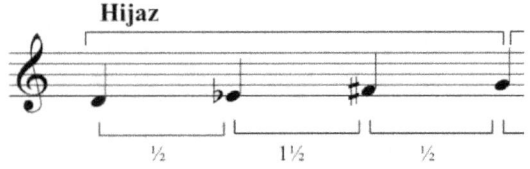

Jins Segah

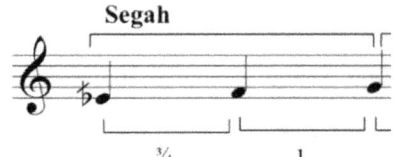

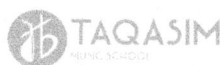

Warm-up Exercises

Warming-up before playing a piece is extremely important. The scales below, *Nahawand* Do and Sol, are written in two octaves. The warm-up is as follows:

- Down/Up risha strokes: 8, 4, 2, 1
- 2 triplets per note
- 1 triplet per note
- Single-note triplet: 3 notes per triplet (e.g. Do, Re, Mi = 1 triplet, Fa, Sol, La = 1 triplet...)

Nahawand Do

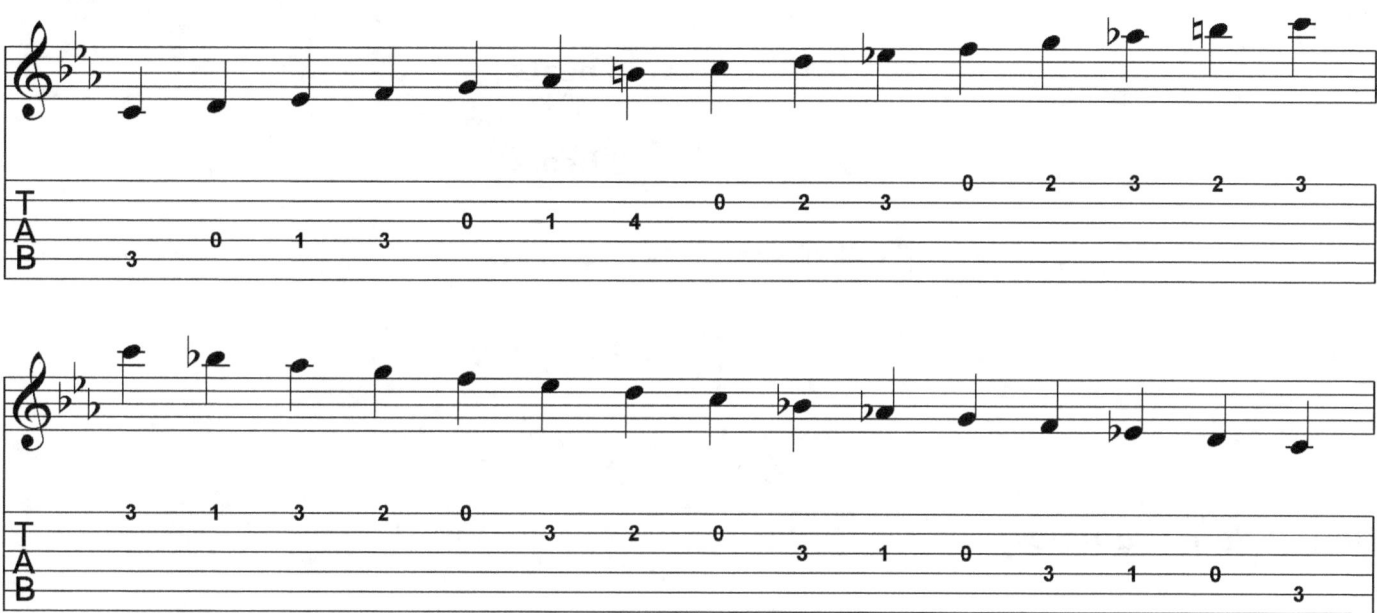

Nahawand Sol

Notice that one octave of Maqam *Hijaz* Re can be found within *Maqam Nahawand* Sol (2 octaves).

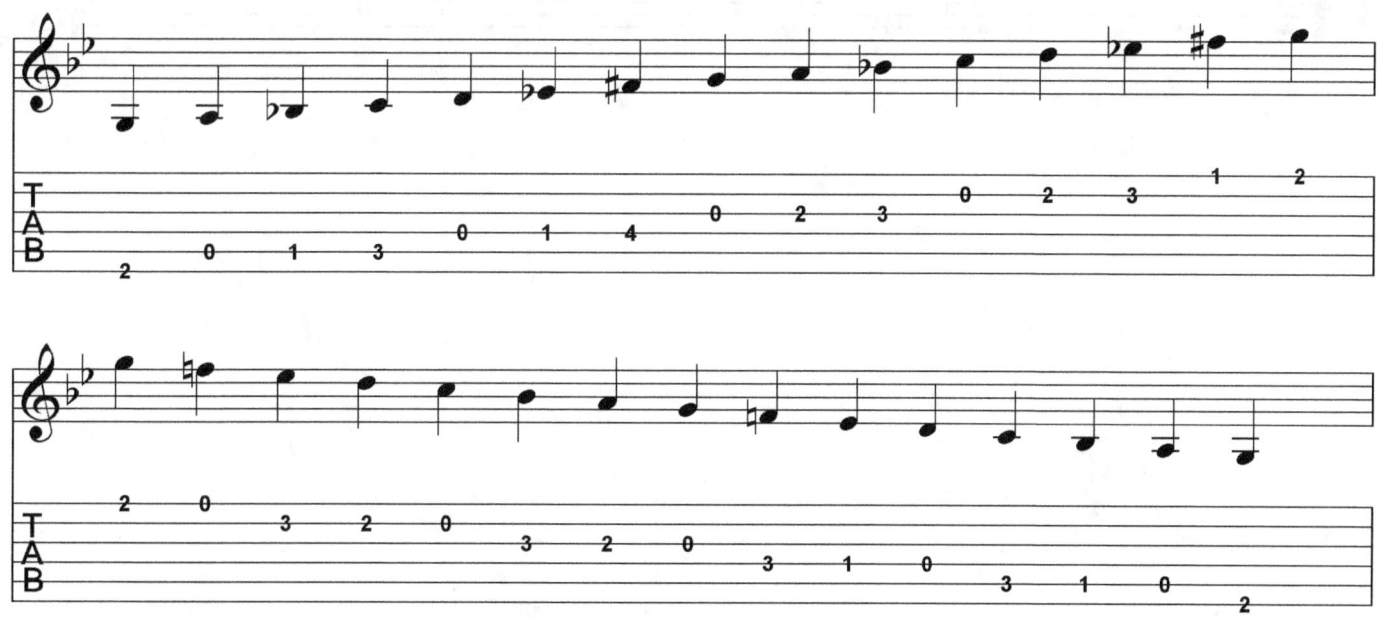

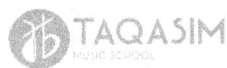

The Dotted Note

Note values can be changed by adding a dot beside the note head as seen here → ♩. ♩. ♪.

This is called a dotted note.

If a dot is added to any note then the note is lengthened by ½ its original value/time.

For example: Since the quarter-note is 1 beat long then a dotted quarter-note will be lengthened by ½ a beat, because ½ of 1 is 1/2.

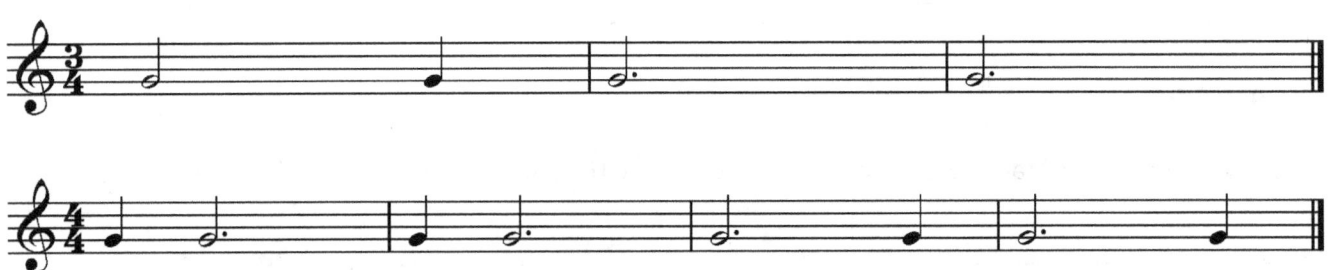

Dotted Note Examples

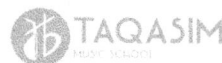

Dotted Note Exercise – *Kurd* La

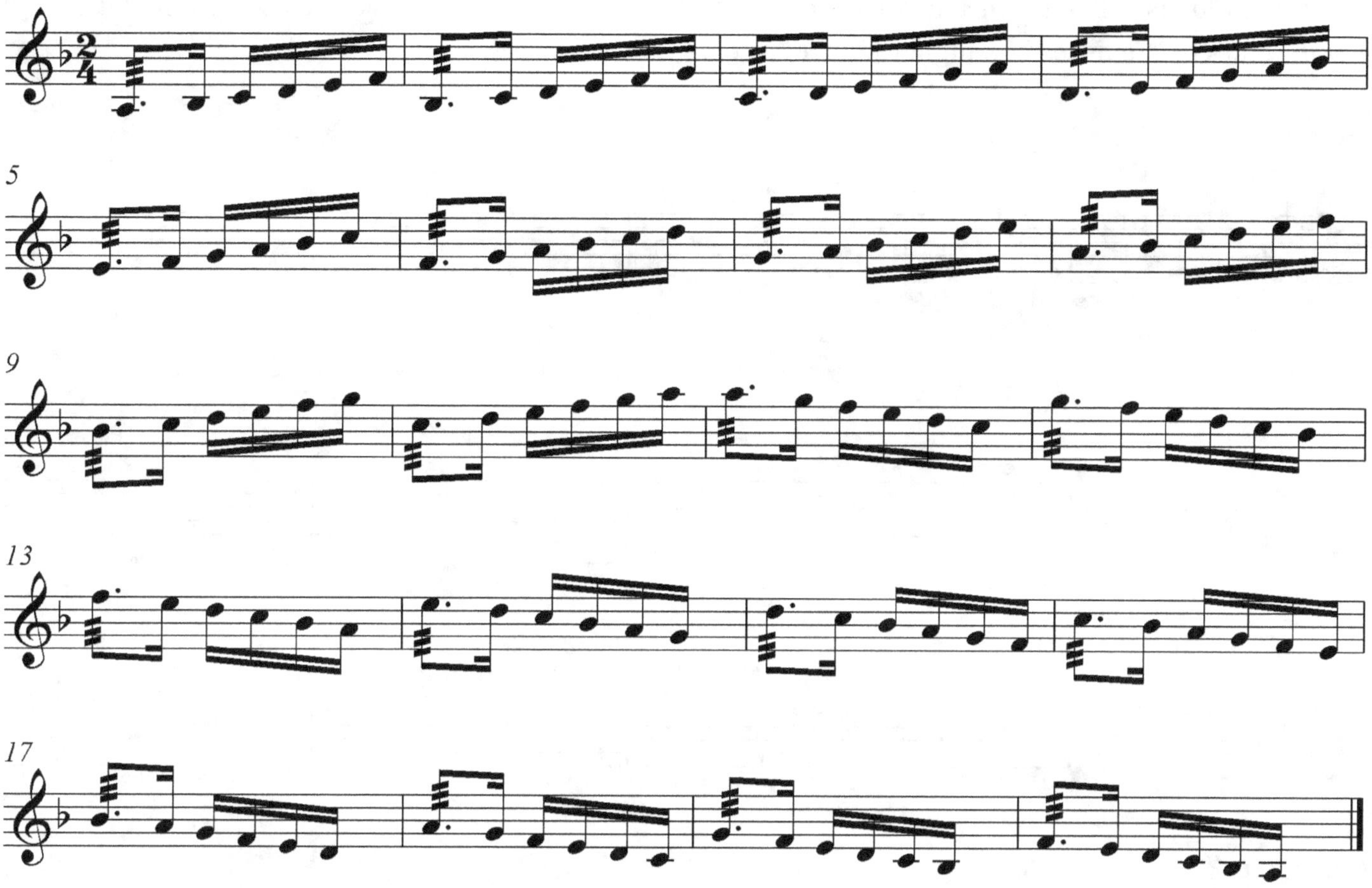

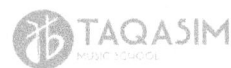

Qarar and Jawab

Playing the same note on two different octaves is a common form of ornamentation in Arabic music. This technique is called *qarar* and *jawab*. *Qarar* refers to the notes of a lower octave/pitch while *jawab* refers to the notes of a higher octave/pitch.

Exercise 1

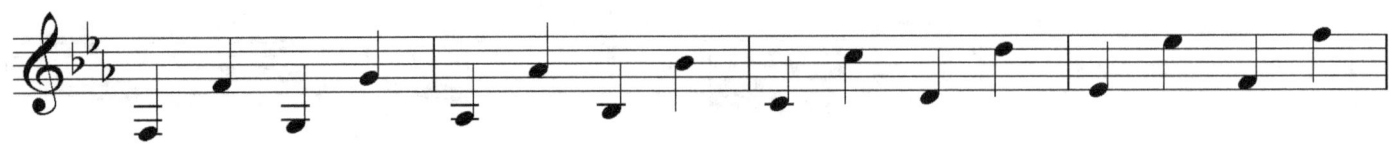

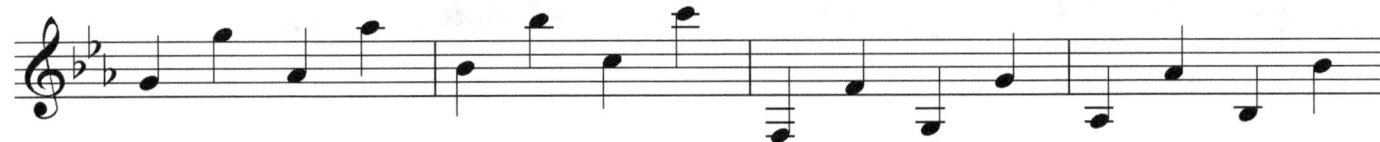

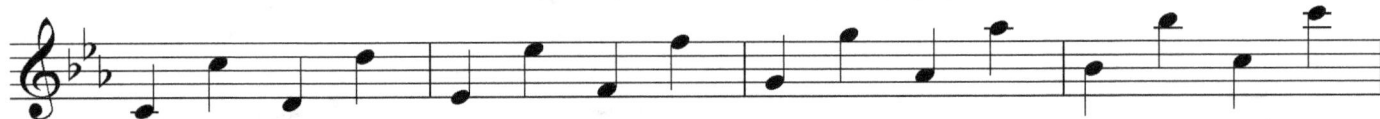

Exercise 2

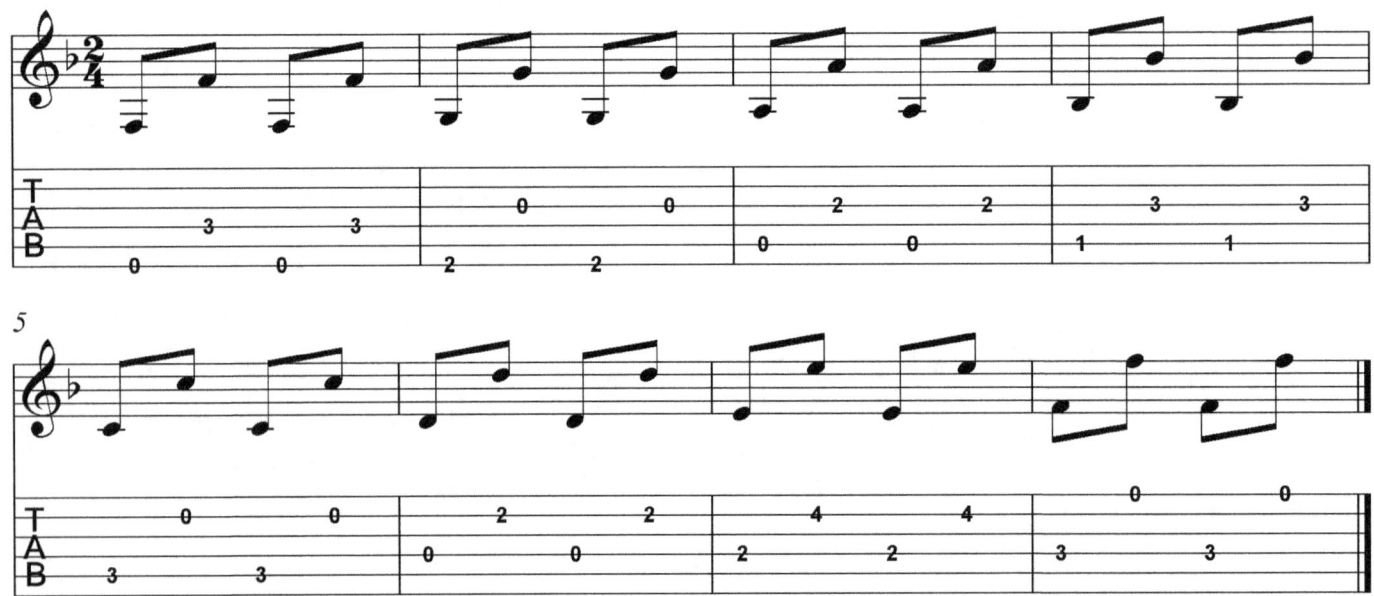

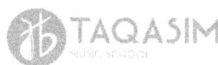TAQASIM

Arpeggio and Triplets

An *arpeggio* is a combination of three separate notes within a scale. These notes can be played in ascending or descending order. The notes are always played in a specific order. The order is: 1st, 3rd and 5th note. The first note determines what the following notes in the arpeggio will be.

For example, there are several combinations of notes that create arpeggios in *Nahawand* Do. Some of those sequences are: Do, Mi, Sol where Do is the 1st note or Re, Fa, La, where Re is the 1st note determining the sequence of the notes that follow.

The following is a set of notations representing ascending and descending arpeggio scales written as triplets. These represent arpeggios found in *Maqam Nahawand* Do.

The symbols used on the score indicate which direction the risha is meant to strike each note.

- Symbols used:
  - ∧ = down-stroke
  - ∨ = up-stroke

Arpeggio and Triplet Exercise

This exercise focuses on combining arpeggios with triplets using two octaves.

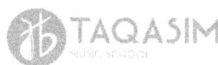

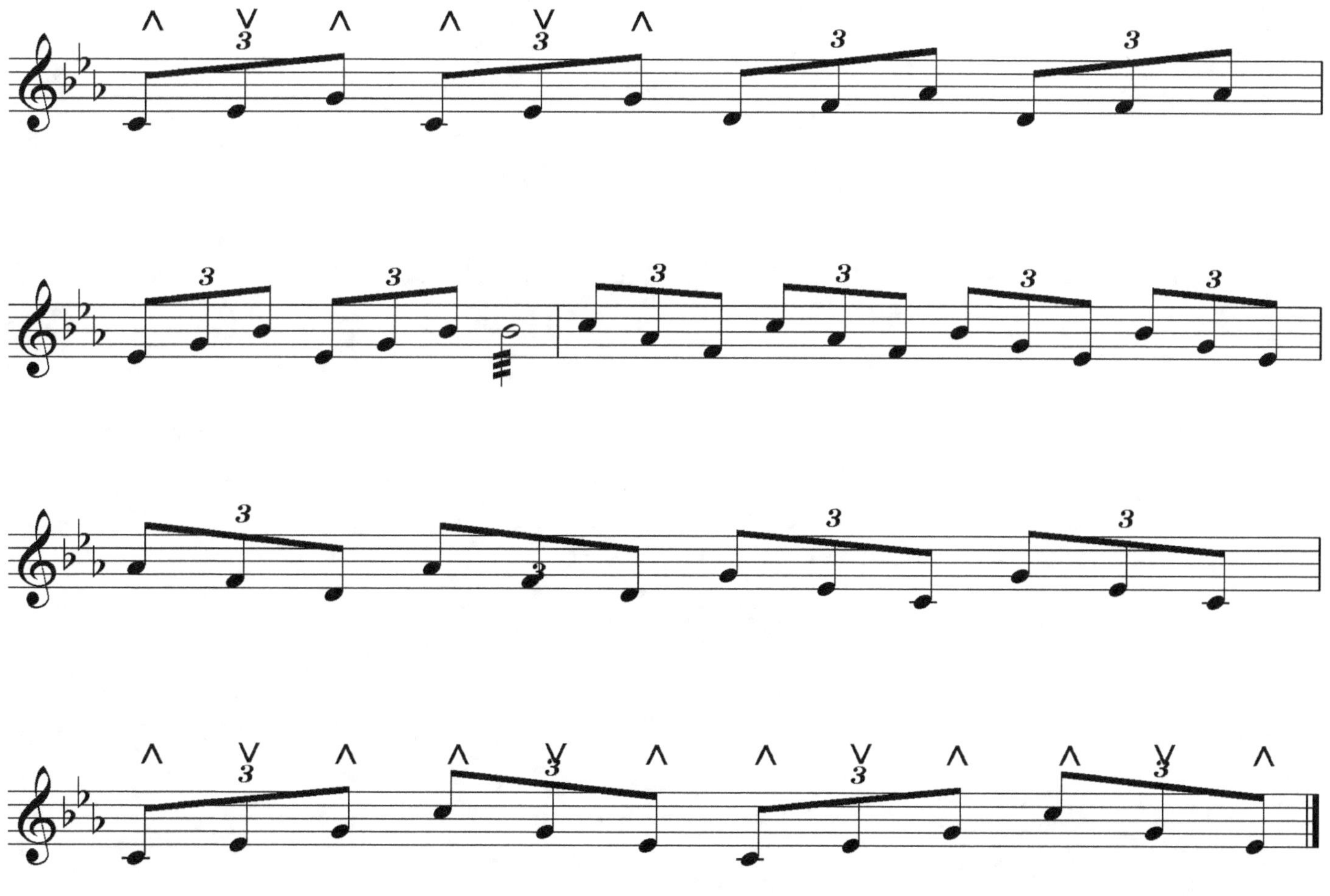

33

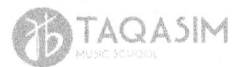

Qarar & Jawab Triplet Exercises

The exercises below combine two important techniques that have been covered: *qarar* and *jawab*, and triplets. As in the previous exercise, the symbols used on the score indicate which direction the risha is meant to strike each note. This pattern continues throughout the exercise.

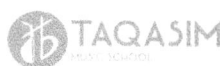

Exercise 1

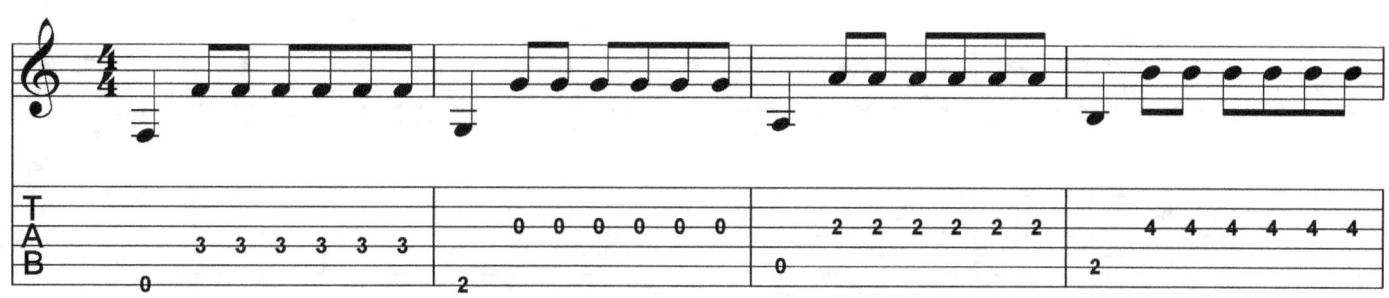

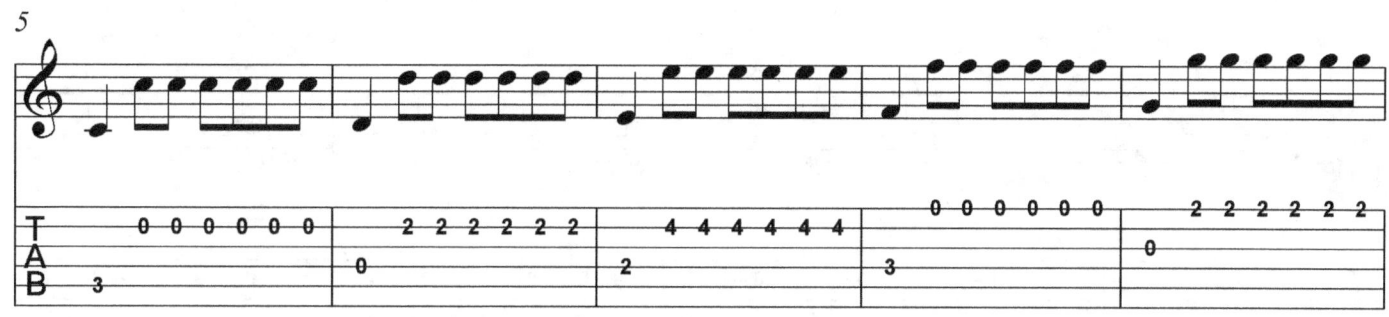

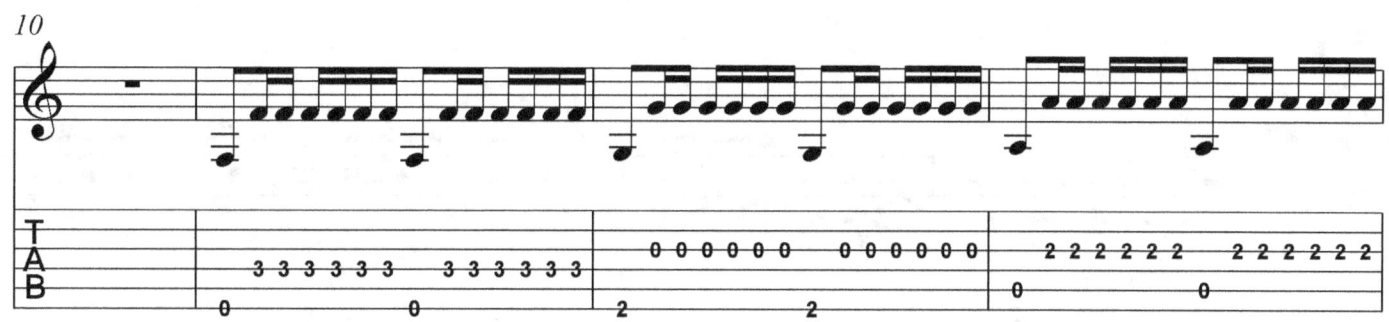

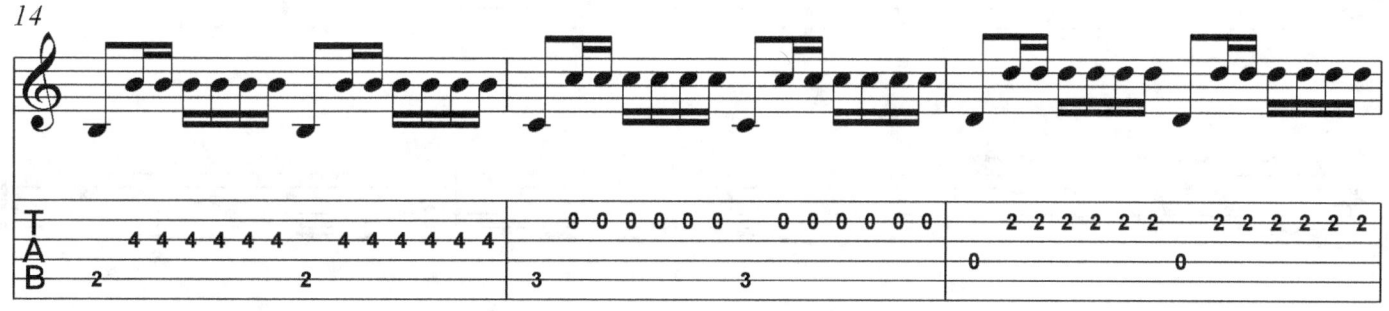

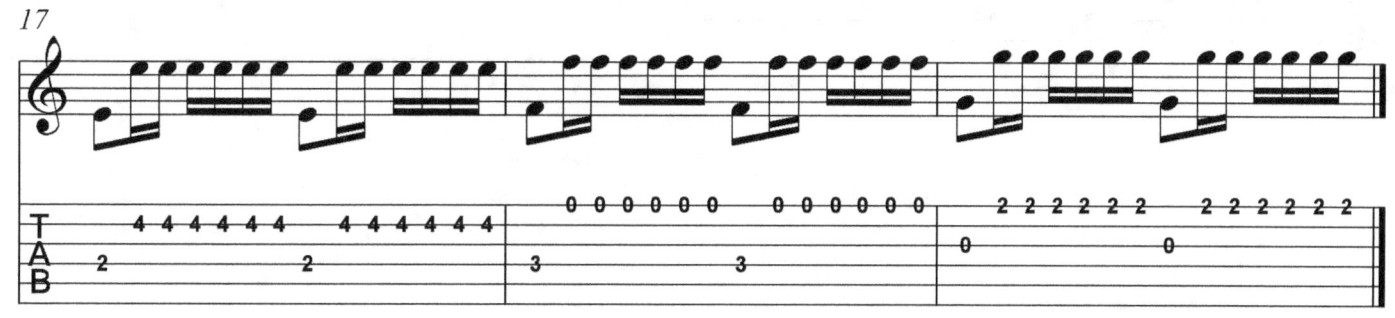

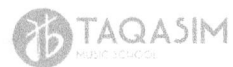

Exercise 2

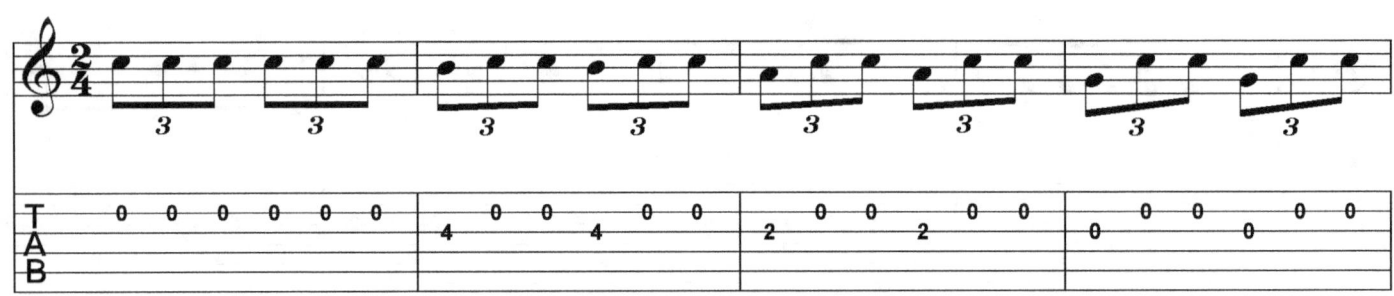

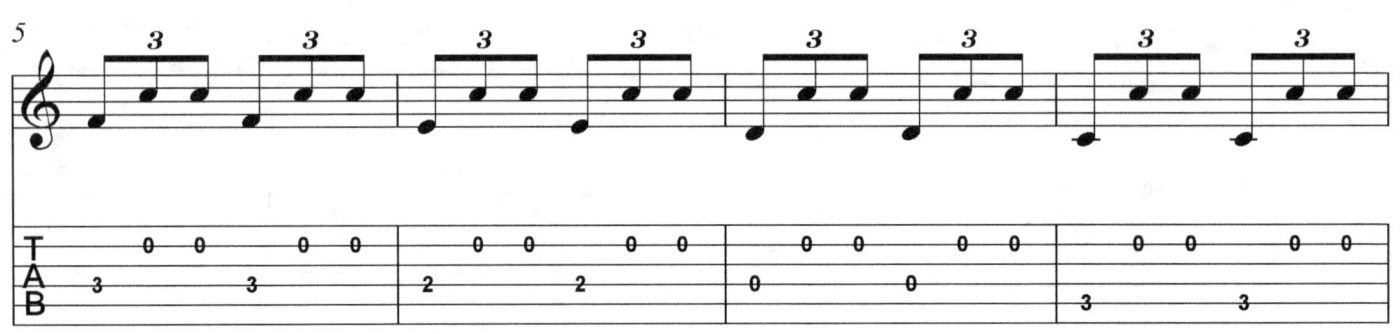

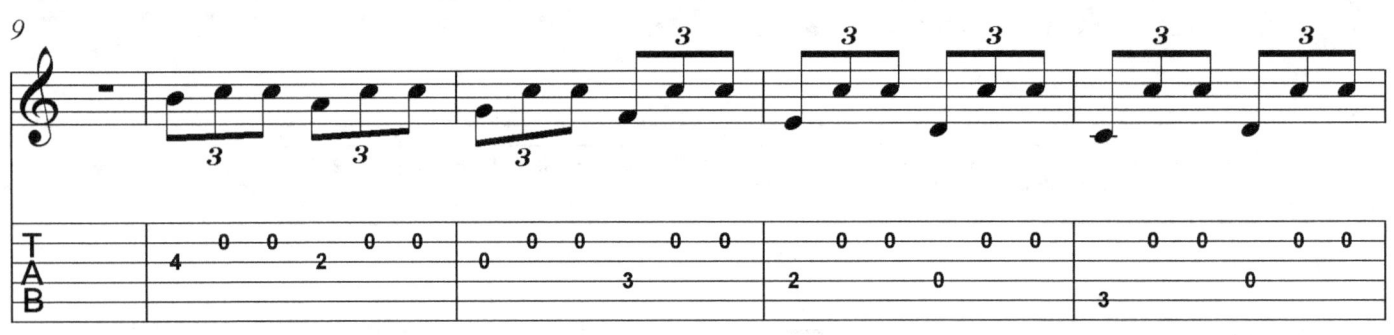

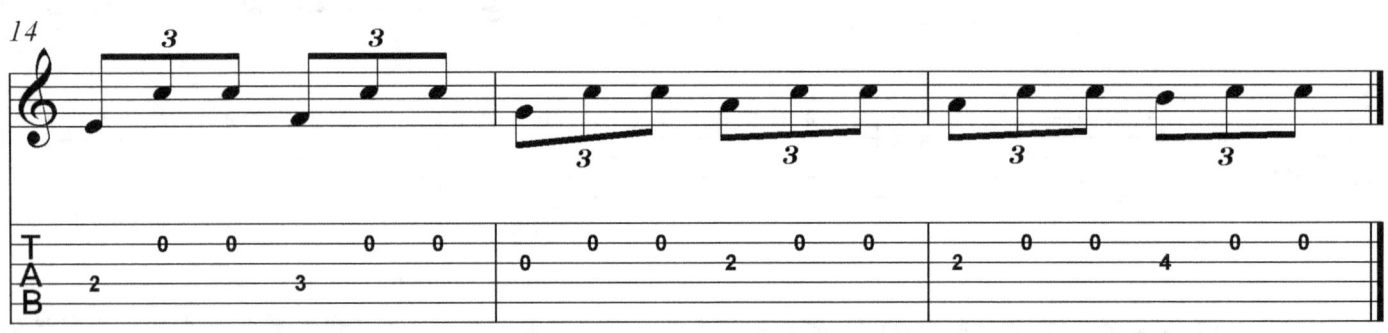

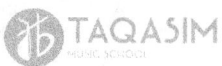

Maqams Nahawand – **Played on One String**

The scores below illustrate how to play *Maqam Nahawand* on one string using all three positions.

Nahawand **Do – on the 5th string only**

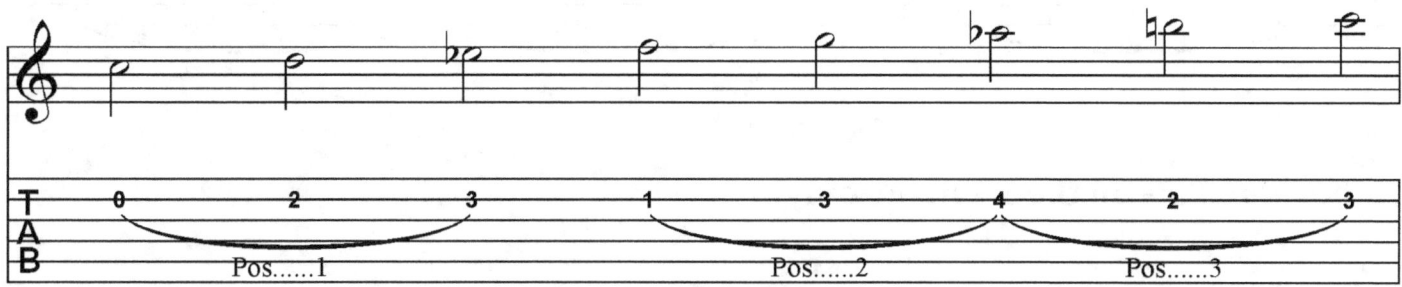

Nahawand **Sol – on the 4th string only**

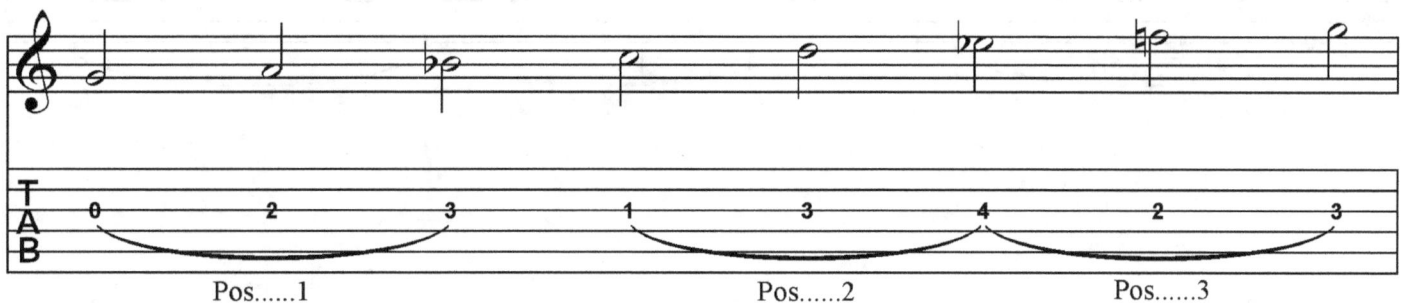

Nahawand **Re – on the 3rd string only**

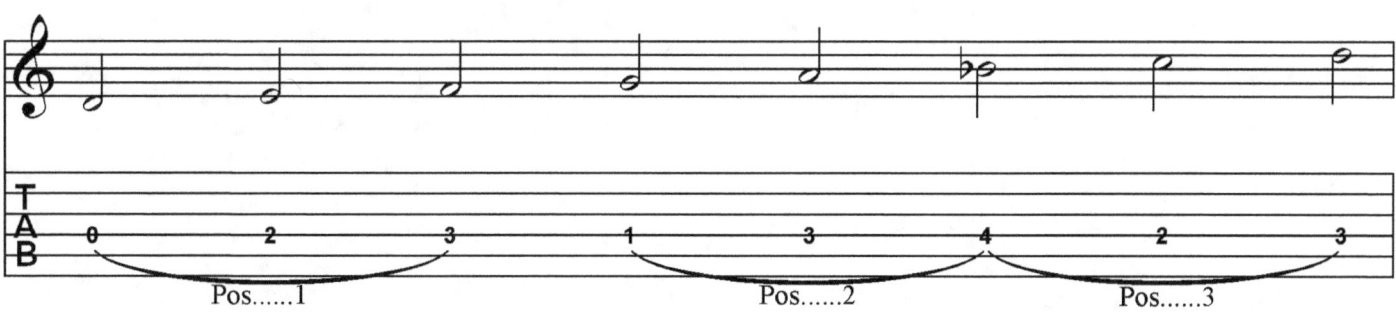

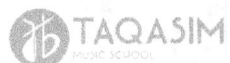

Nahawand La – on the 2nd string only

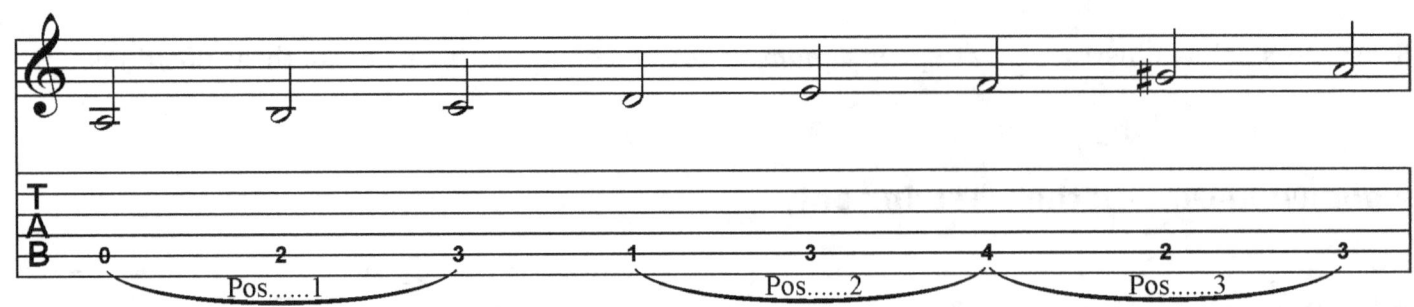

Nahawand Fa – on the 1st string only

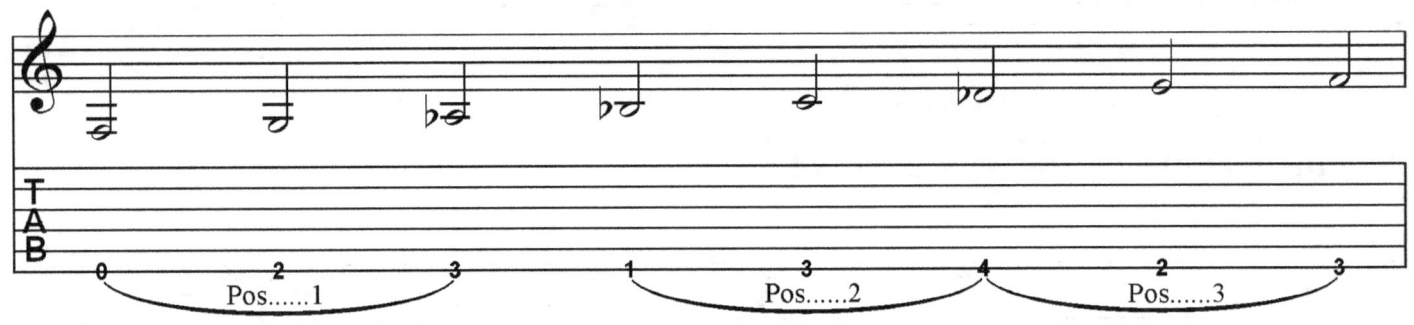

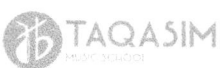

Qari'at al-Finjaan

Qari'at al-Finjaan was written by Mohammad al-Mouji and sung by Egyptian singer *Adul Halim Hafiz.* This piece uses *qarar* and *jawab* (see bars 5 to 11), dotted notes and tremolos. This section is written using *Maqam Kurd.*

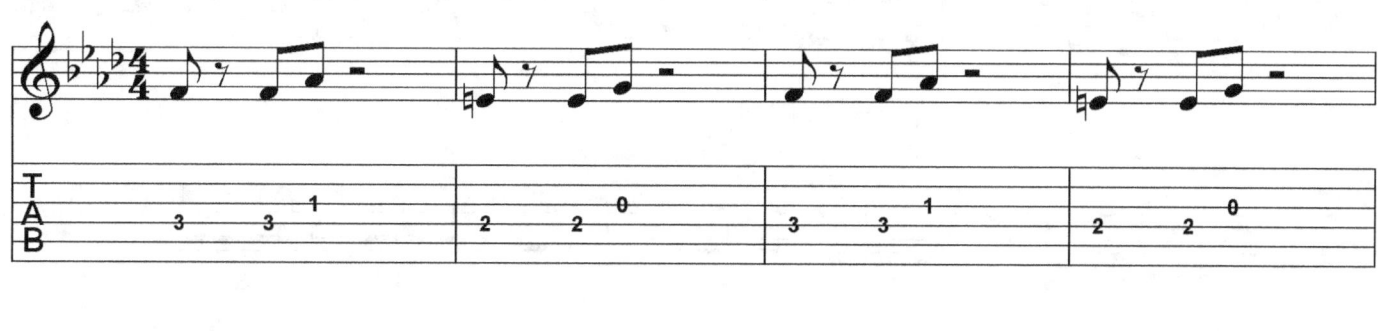

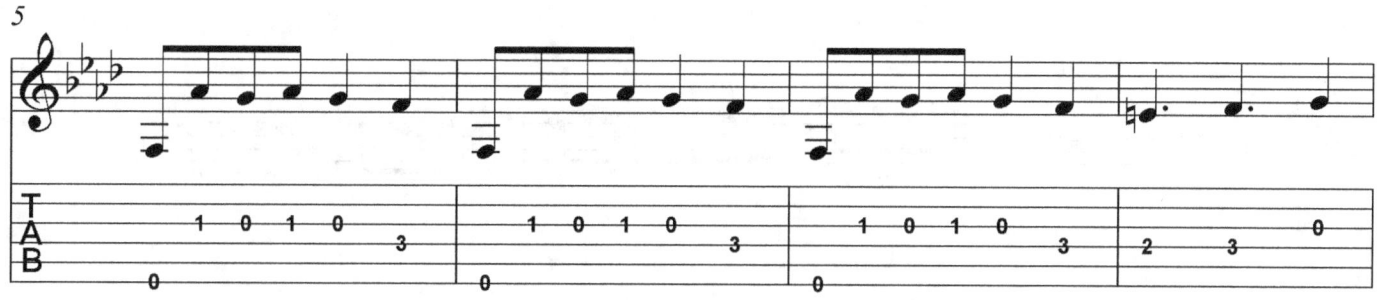

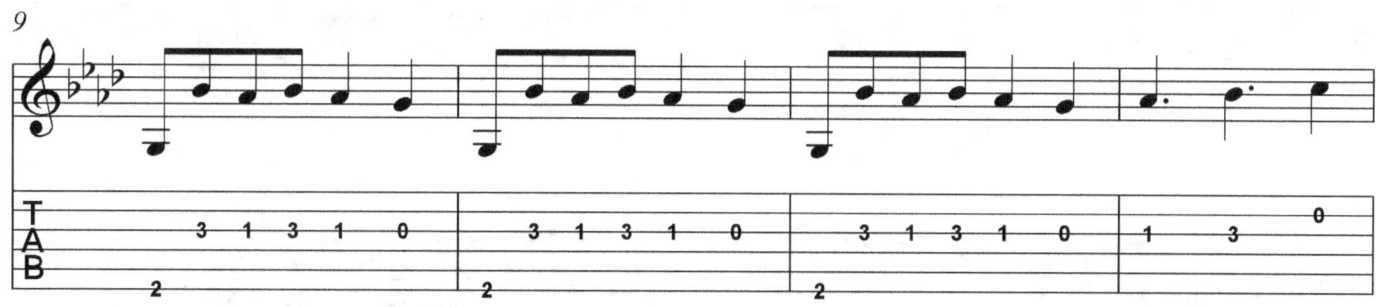

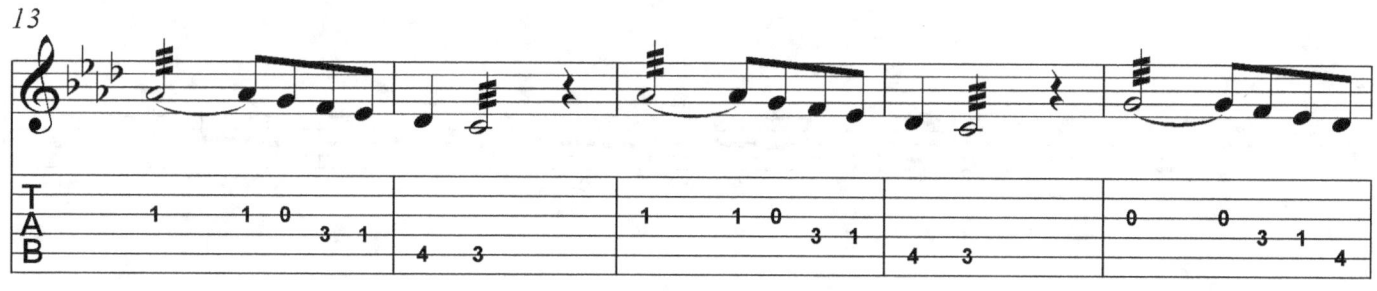

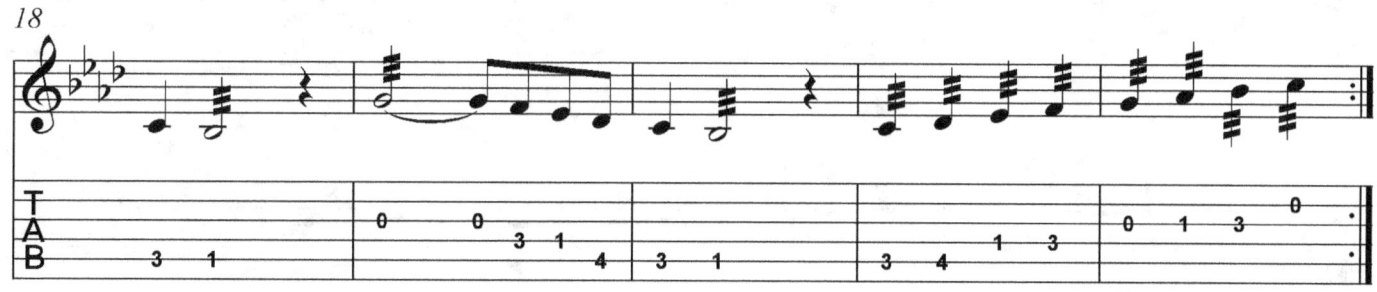

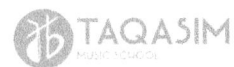

Triplet Exercise – Nahawand (2 Octaves)

Remember: Triplets always use a **down-up-down** movement. The Triplet is one of the Oud's important *risha* techniques and should be played using a **down-up-down** wrist movement.

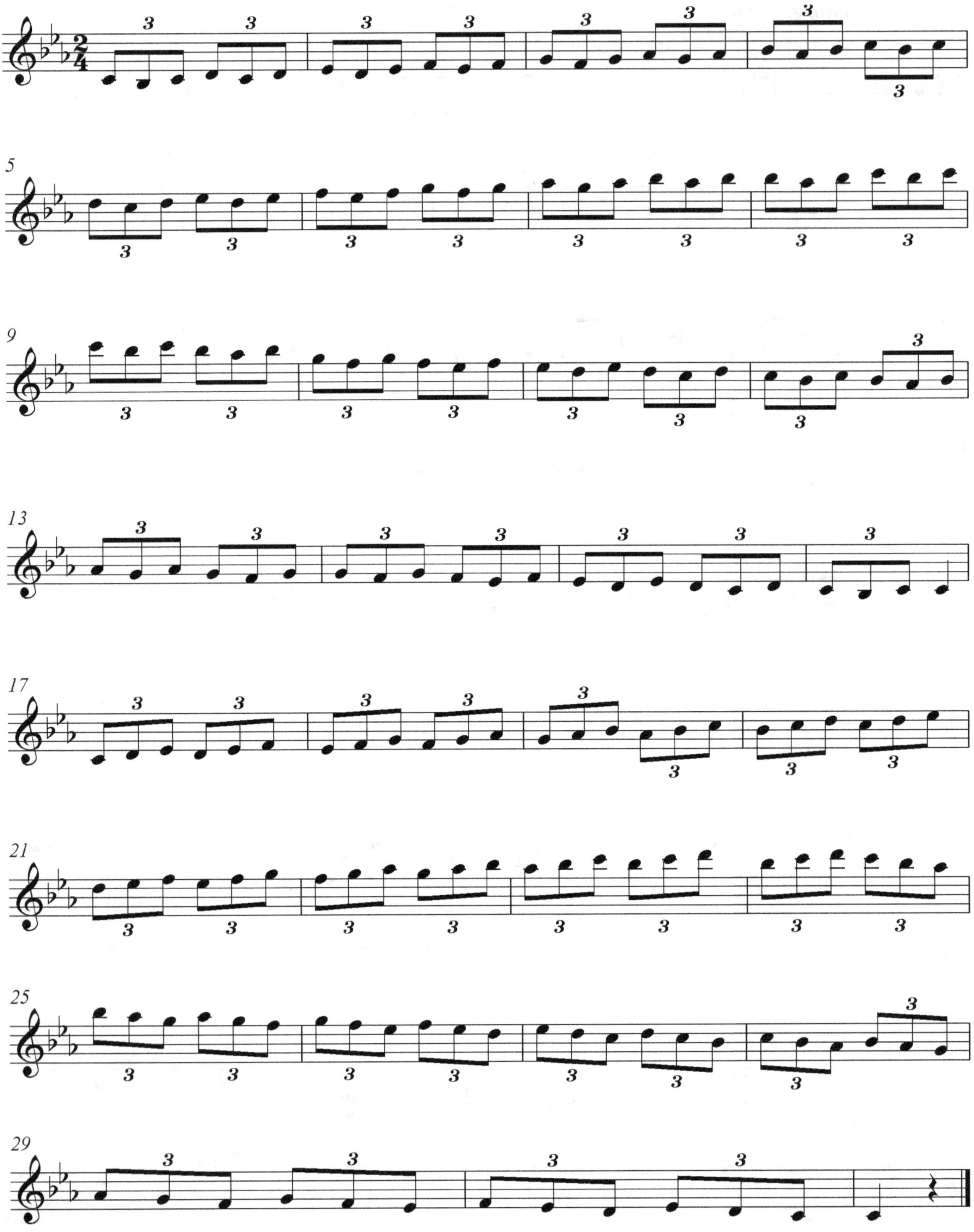

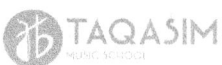

Longa Nahawand (Sol)

This *longa* was written on *Nahawand* Sol, by Turkish composer *Yorgo* Bacanos (1900 – 1977). Notice that triplets are heavily used in this piece.

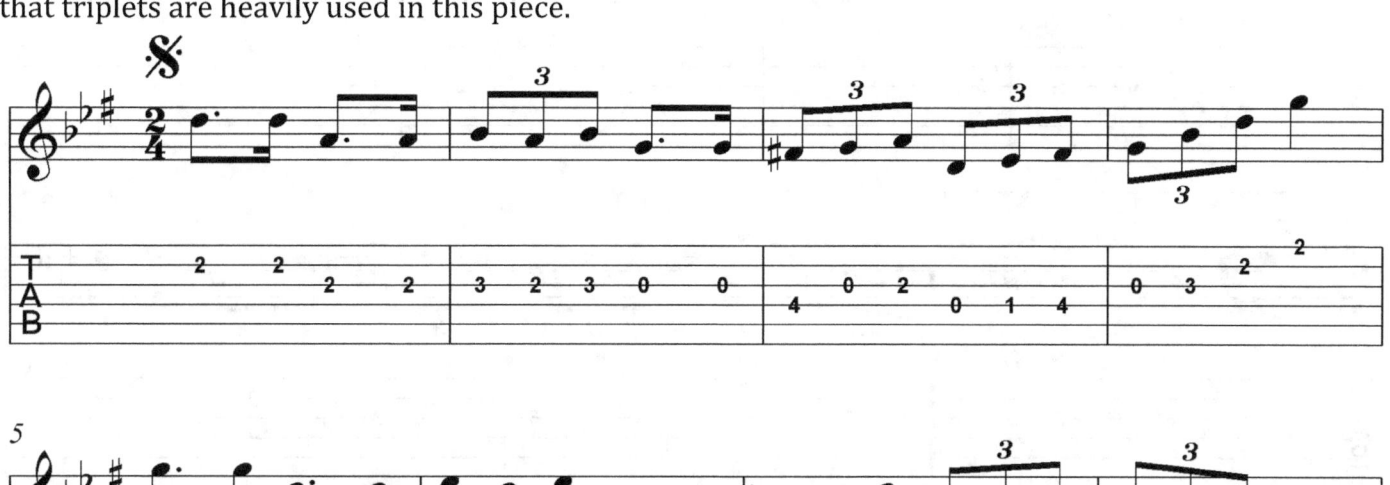

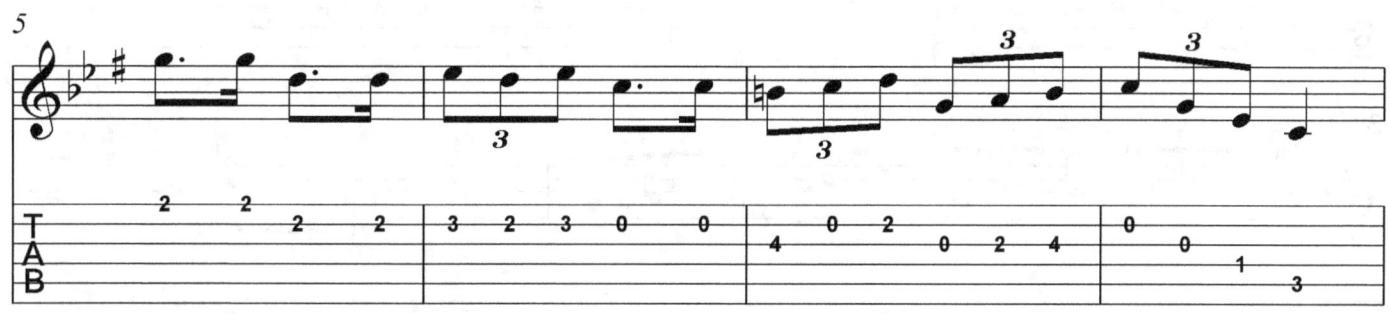

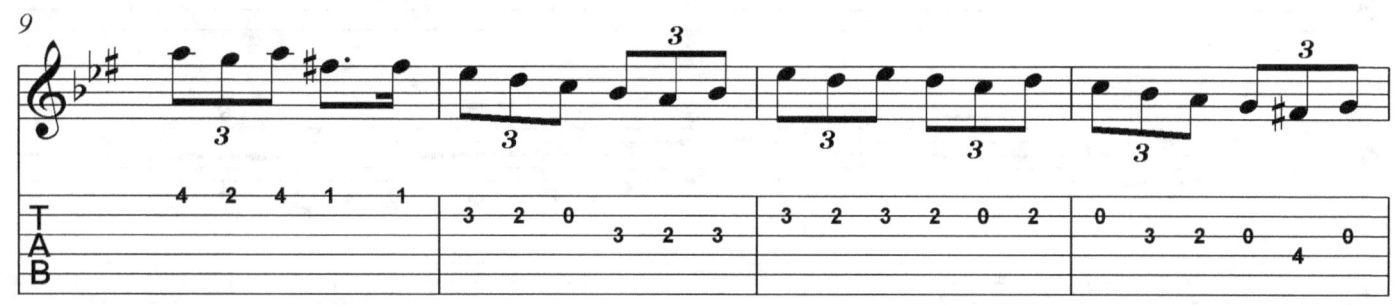

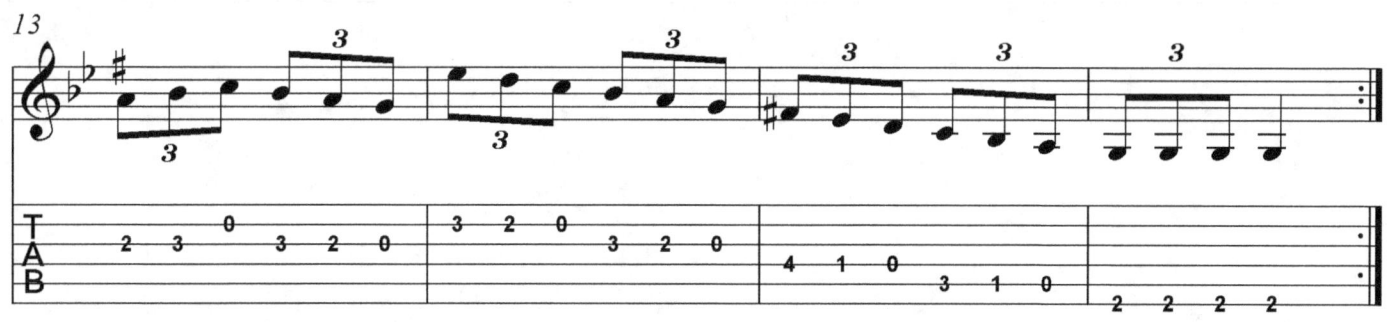

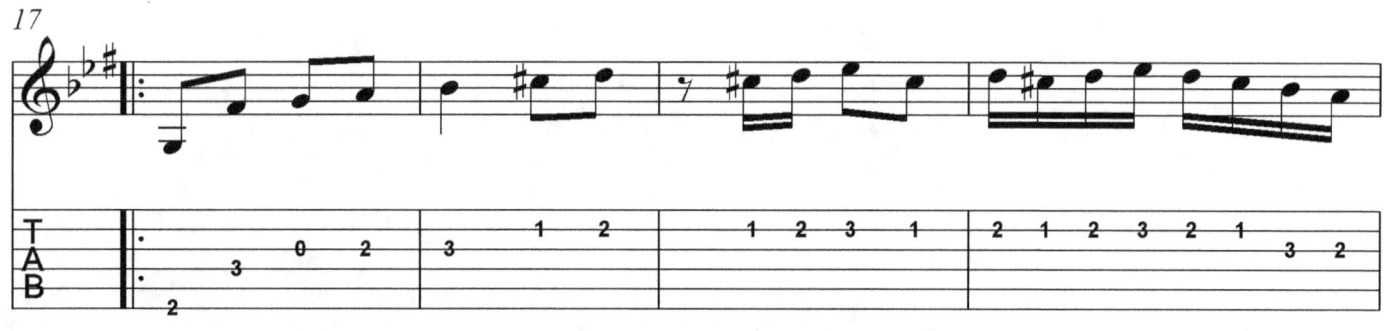

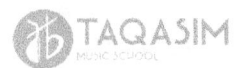

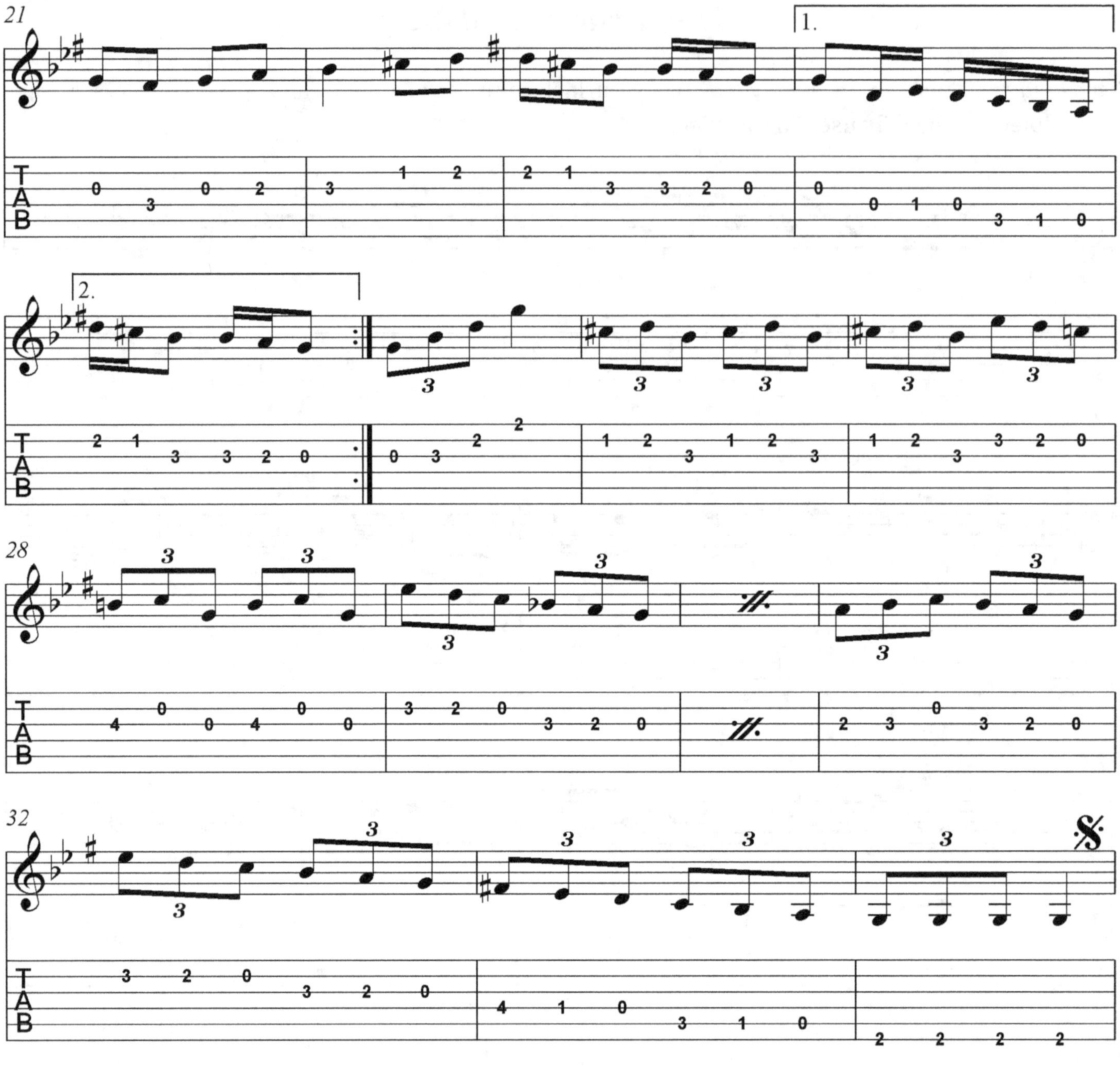

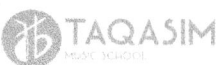

Maqam Ajam – Played on One String

The scores below illustrate how to play *Maqam Ajam* on one string using all three positions.

Ajam Do – on the 5th string only

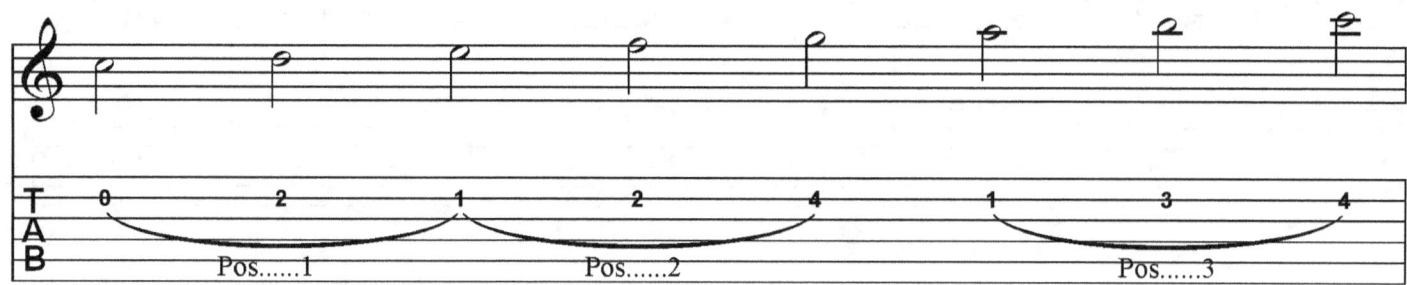

Ajam Sol – on the 4th string only

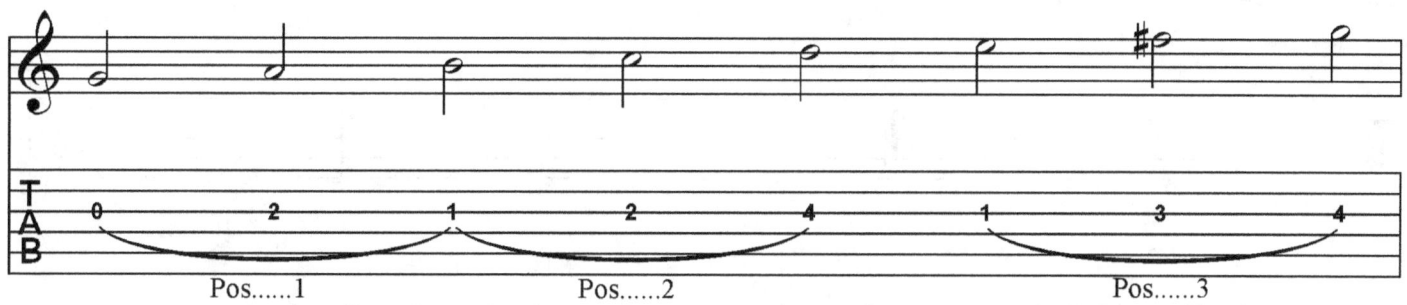

Ajam Re – on the 3rd string only

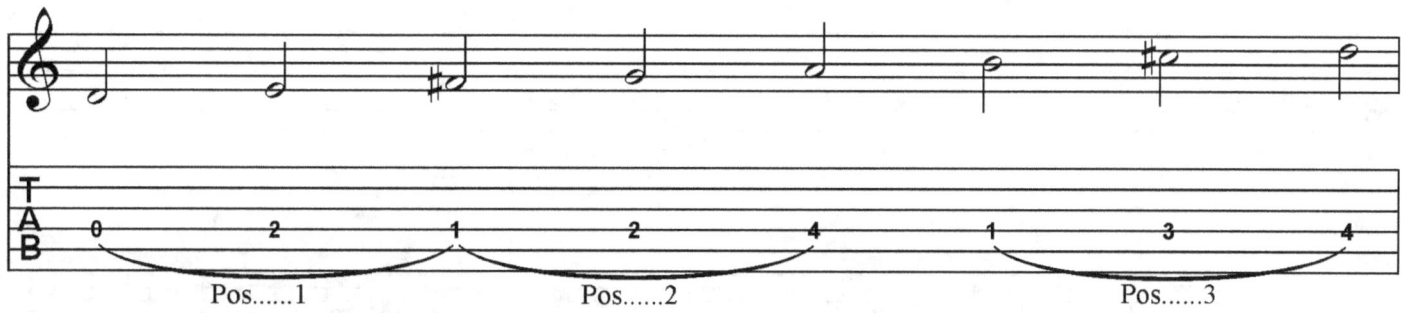

Ajam La – on the 2nd string only

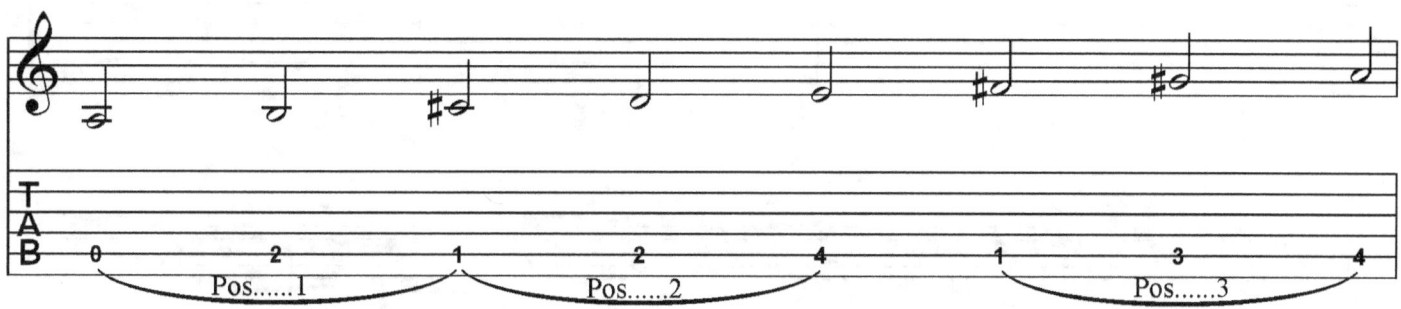

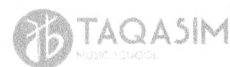

Longa Hijaz Kar Kurd

Longa Hijaz Kar Kurd (notation)

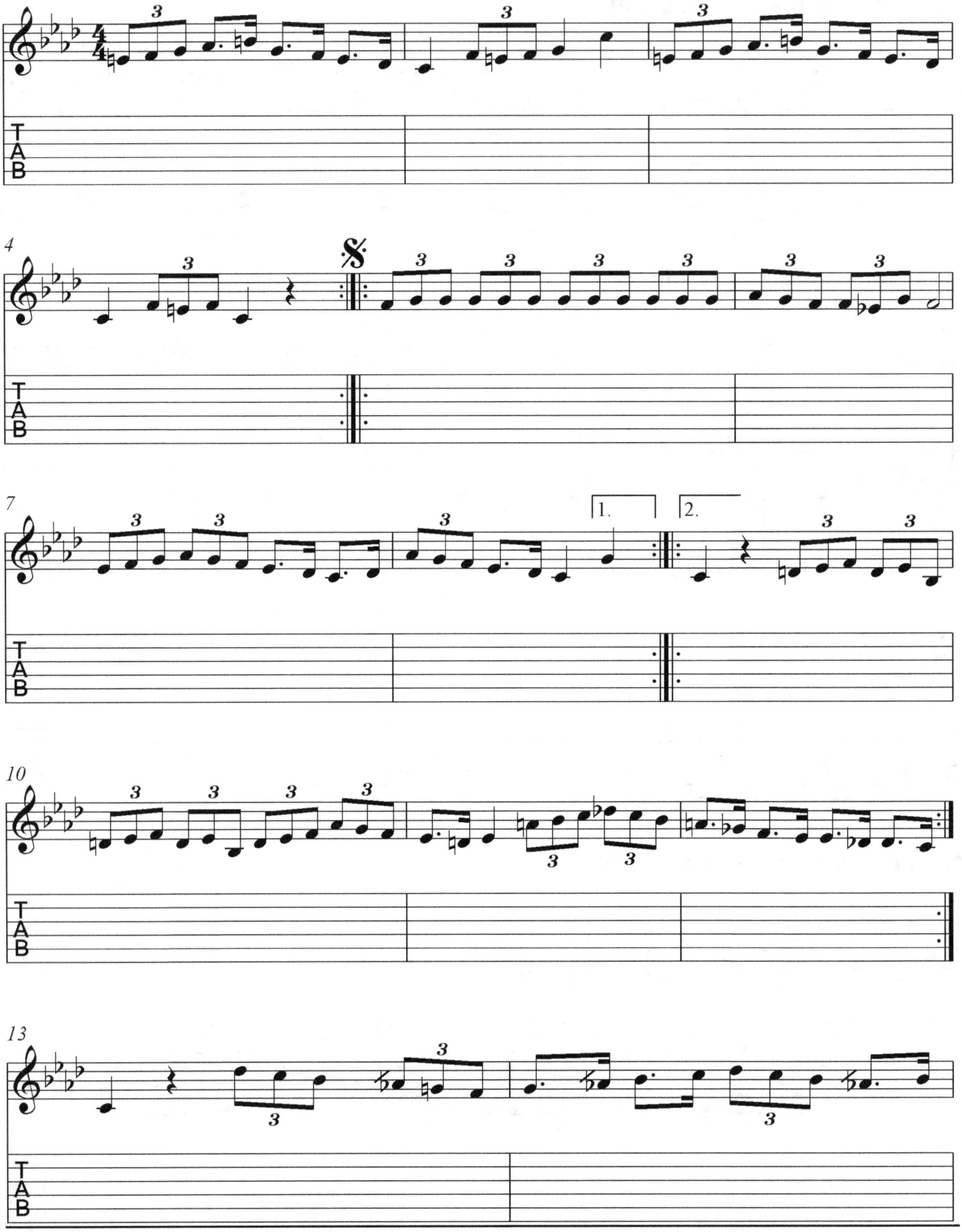

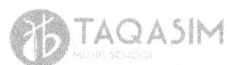

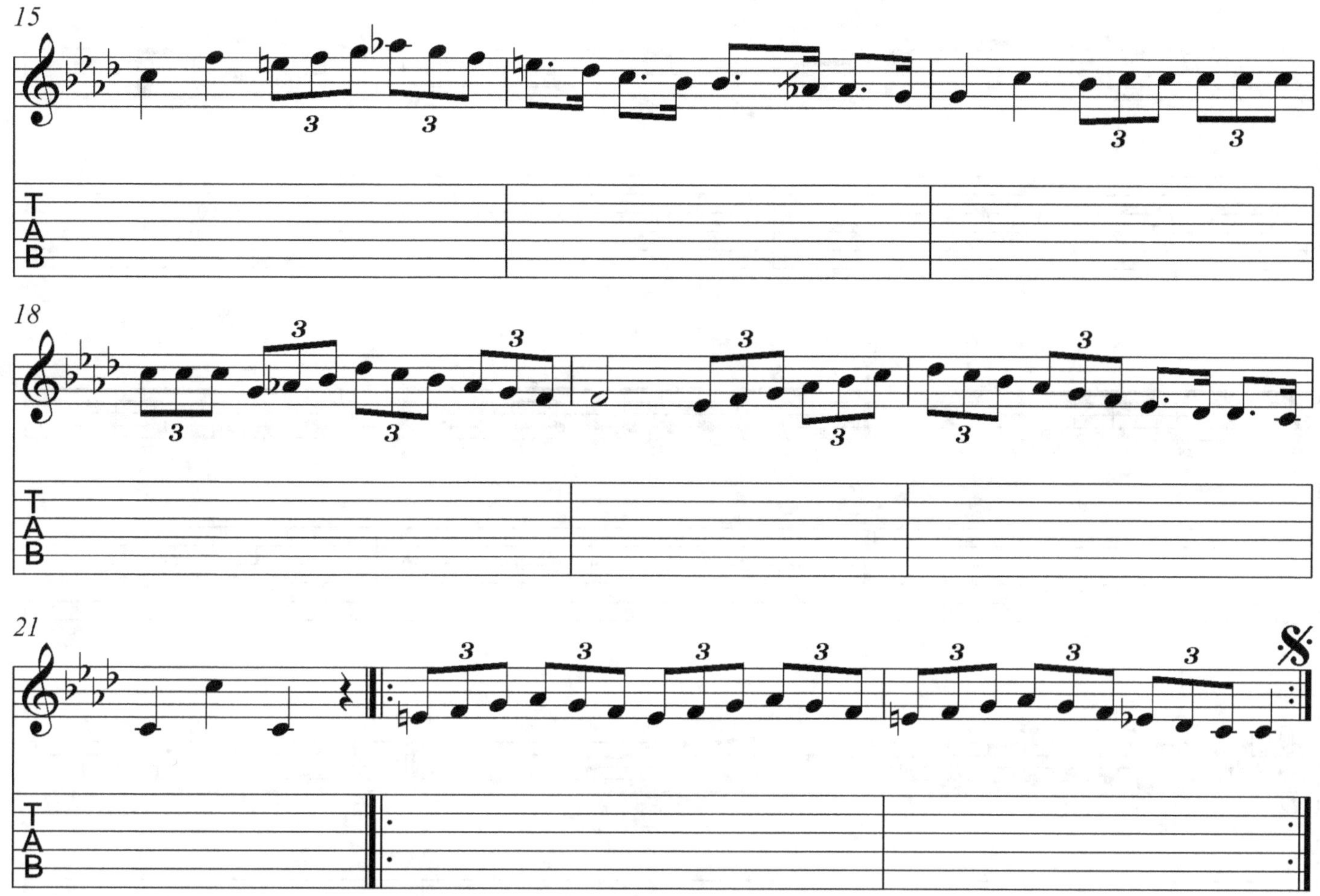

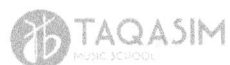

Longa Hijaz Kar Kurd (notation & tablature)

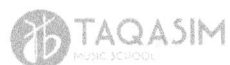

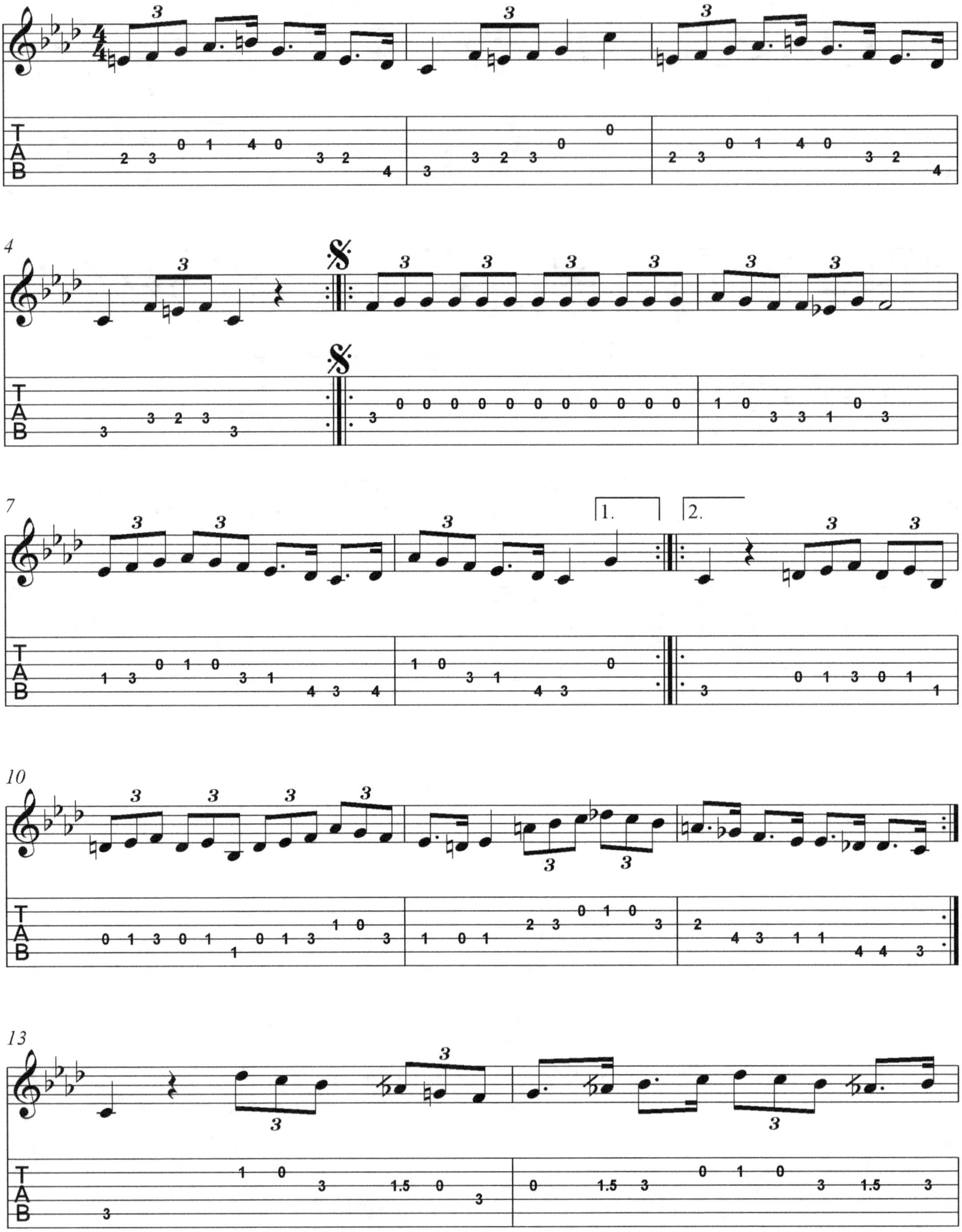

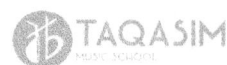

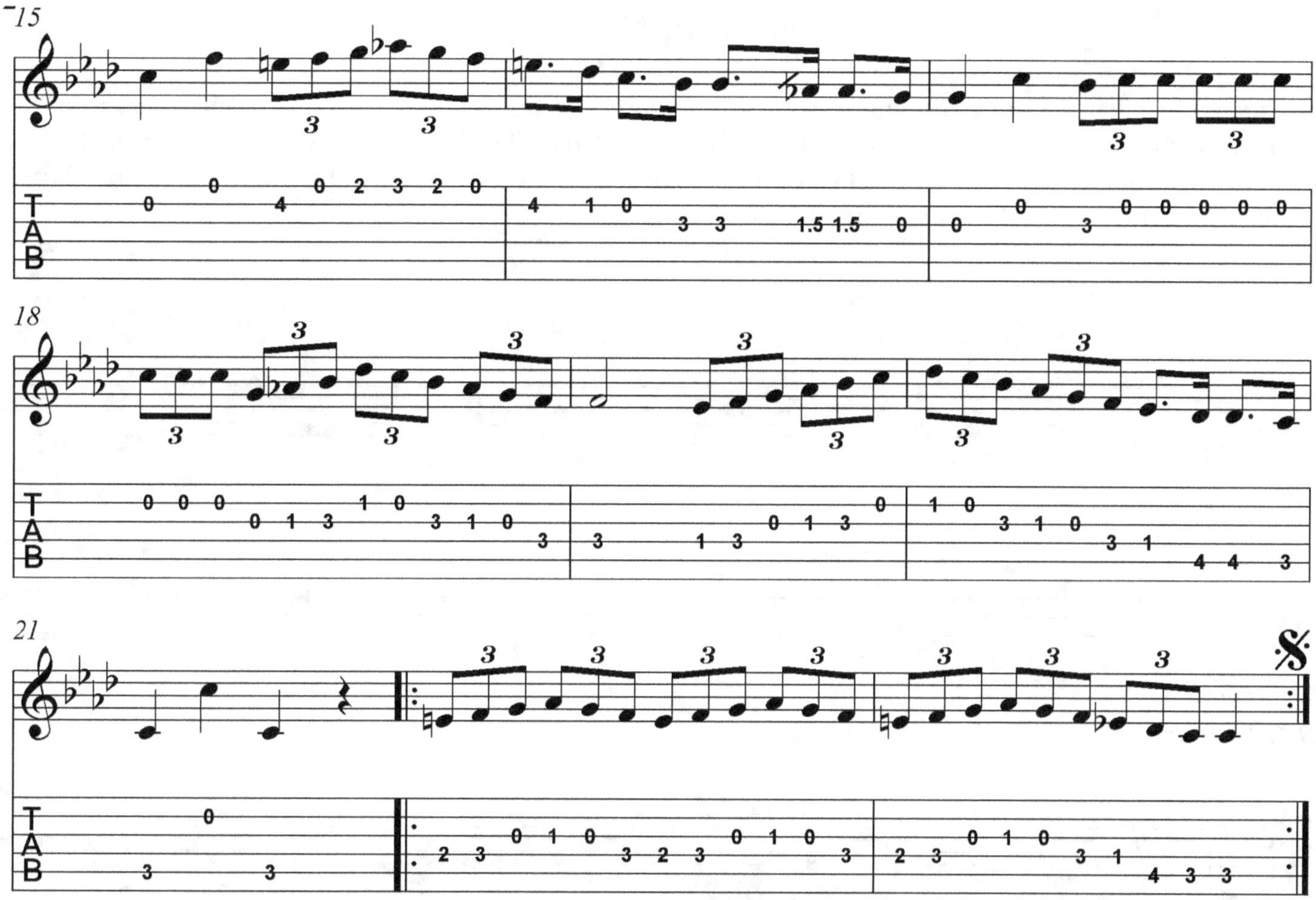

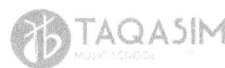

Maqam Nagriz

Maqam Nagriz is a secondary maqam from *Nahawand*. The score below illustrated the maqam in two octaves where both the first and second positions are used. The line drawn in the scale indicates the beginning of the second octave. The last two notes are played on the second position where the thumb of the left-hand is moved towards the middle of the neck.

Nagriz Do

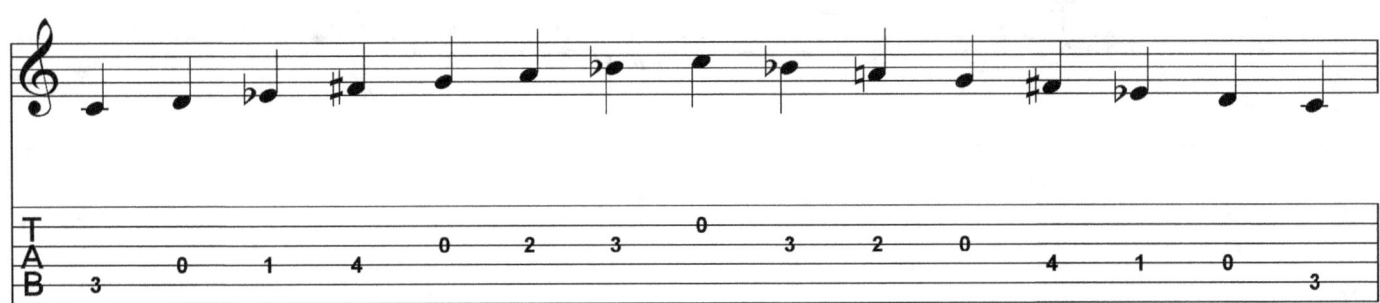

Nagriz Sol

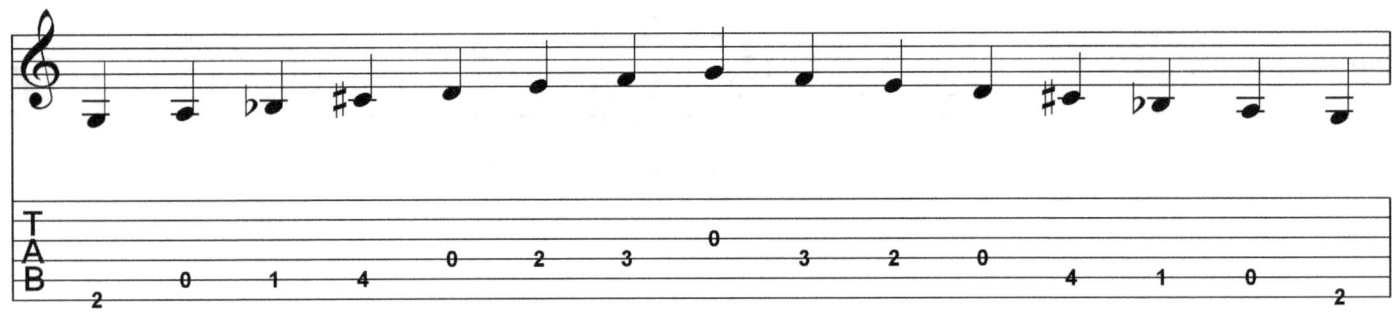

Nagriz Fa – 2 octaves

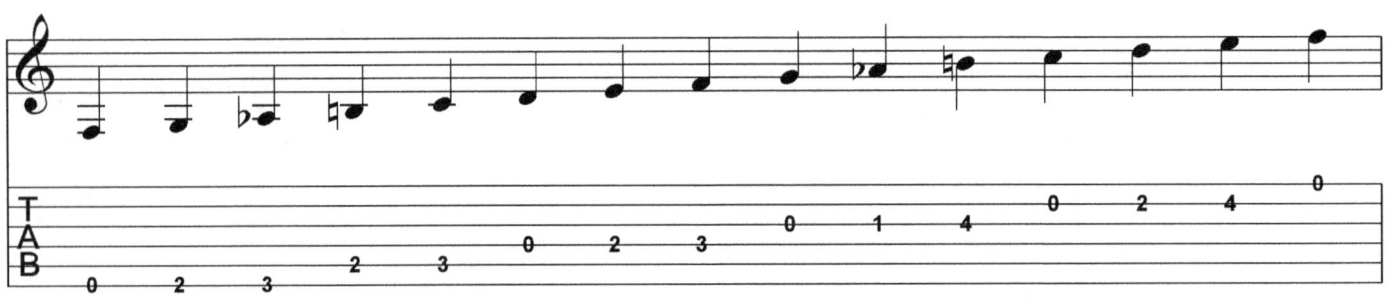

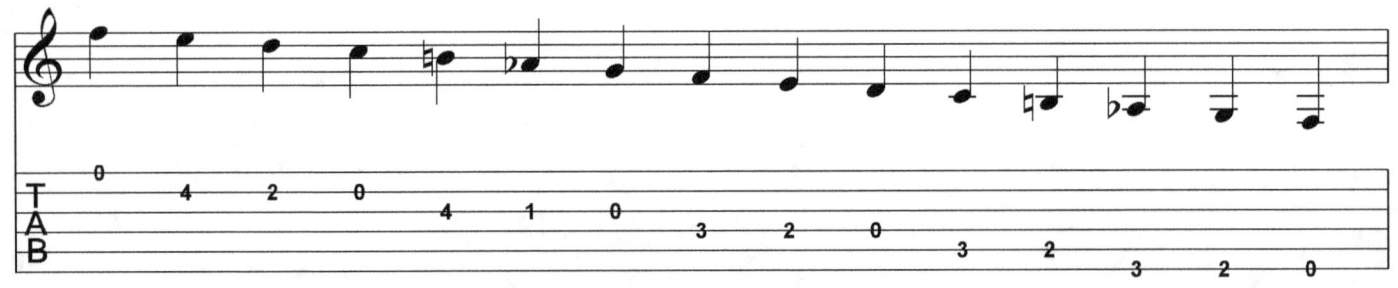

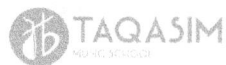

Doulab Nagriz 1

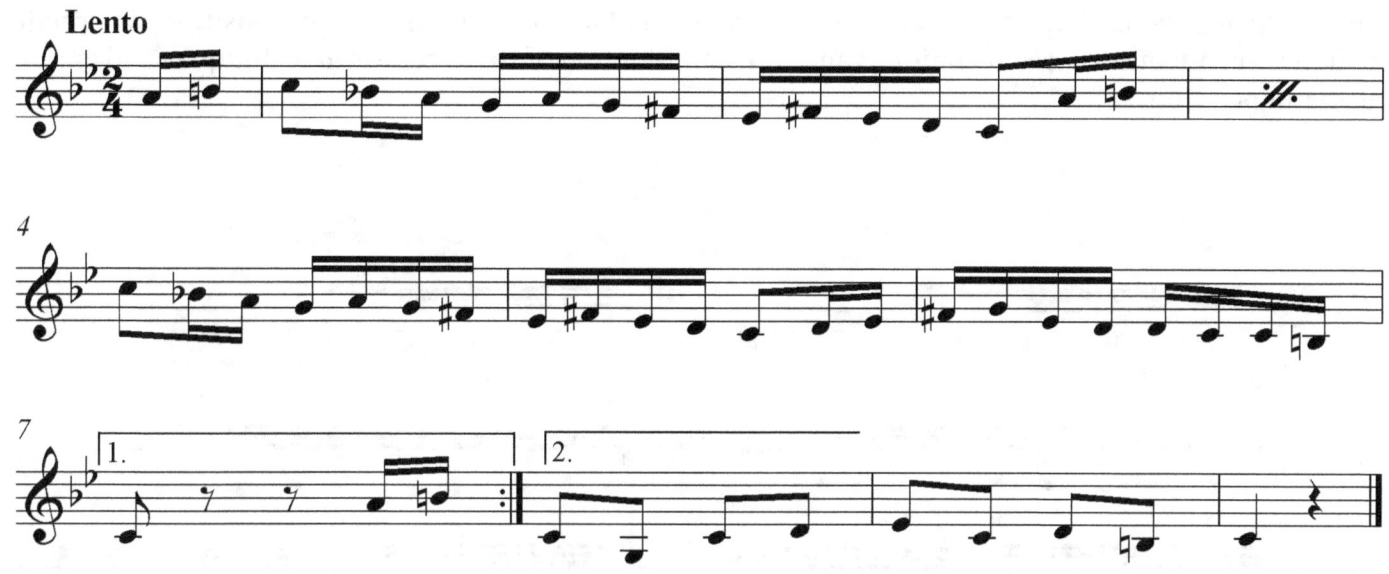

Doulab Nagriz 2 – Iftikirni Umm Kulthoum

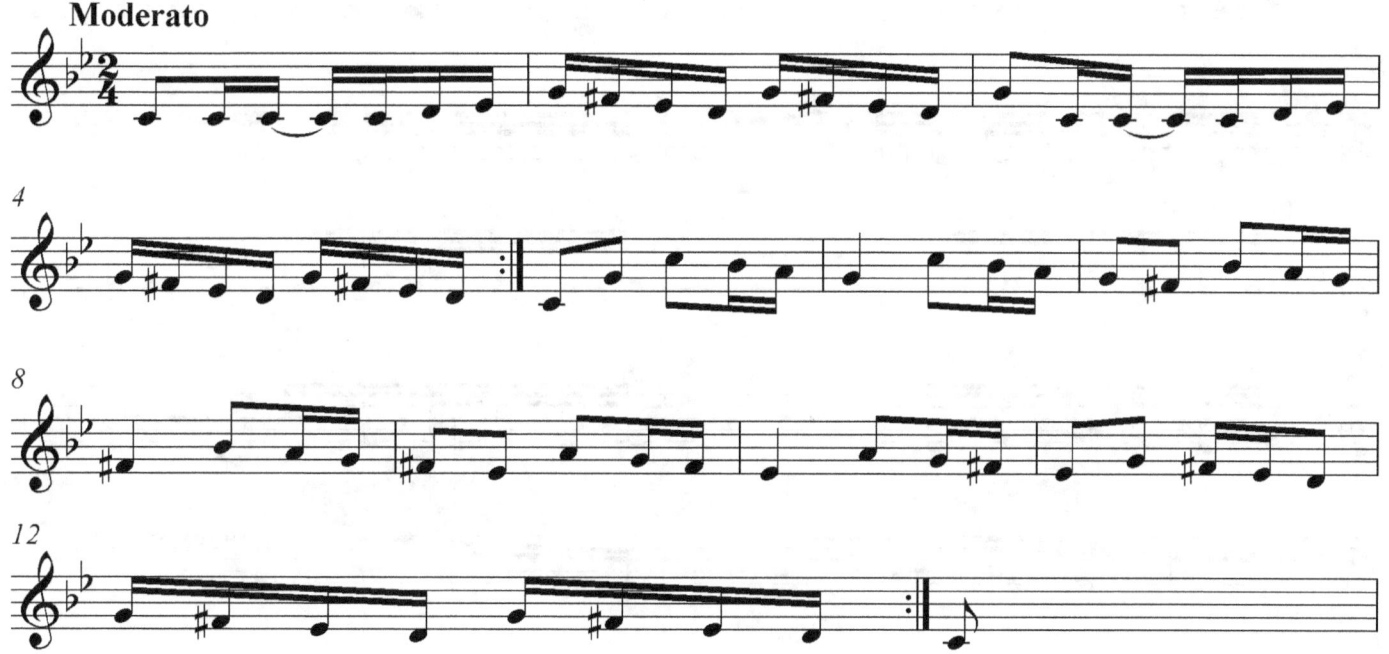

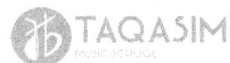

Etude – Maqam Nagriz

This *etude* on *Maqam Nagriz* consists of three parts: 1) *Maqam Nagriz* in the first position. 2) Practice sequences of advanced *risha* techniques and 3) A combination of advanced *risha* techniques and various left-hand positions.

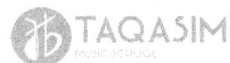

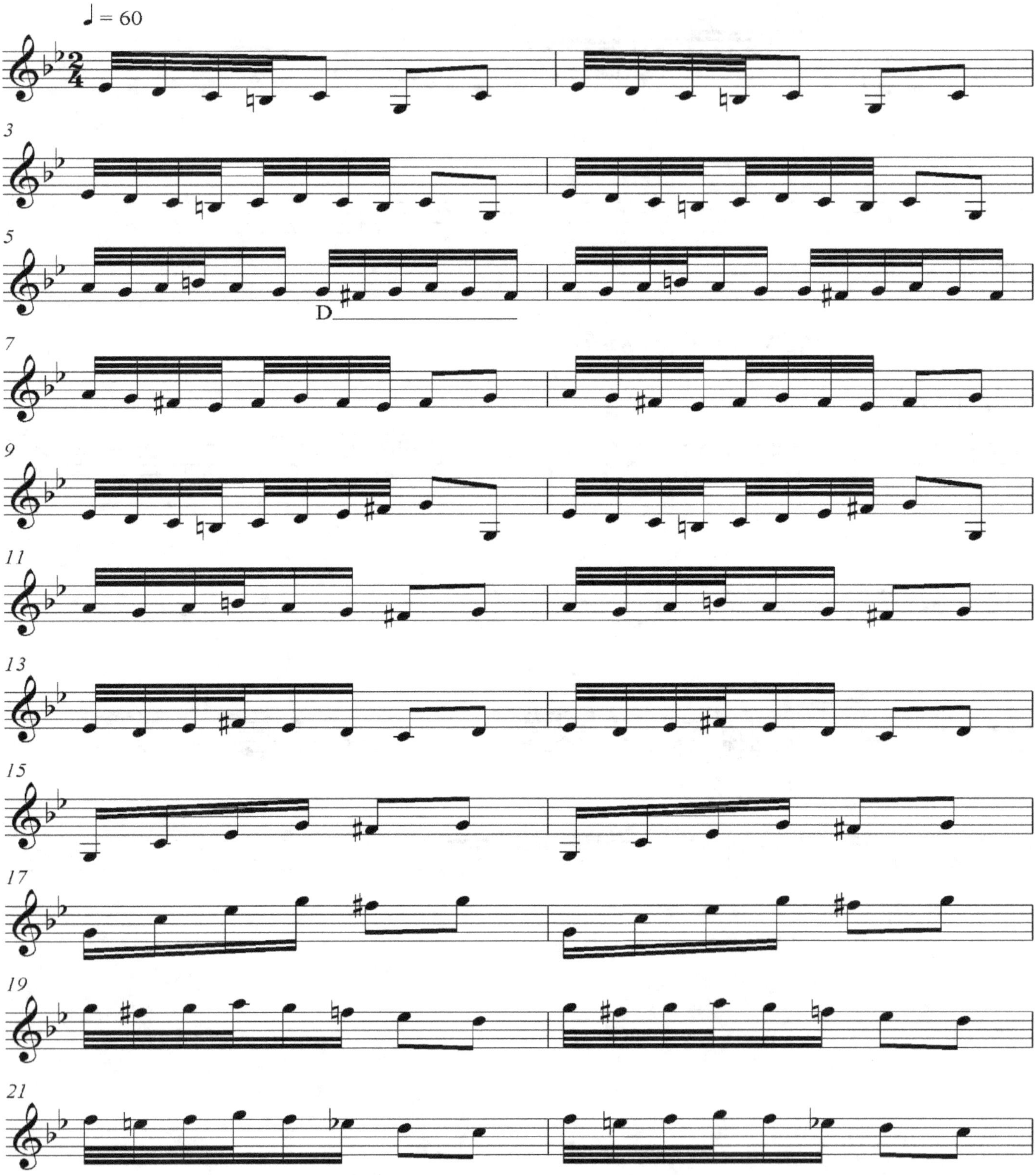

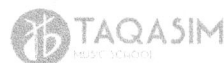

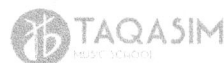

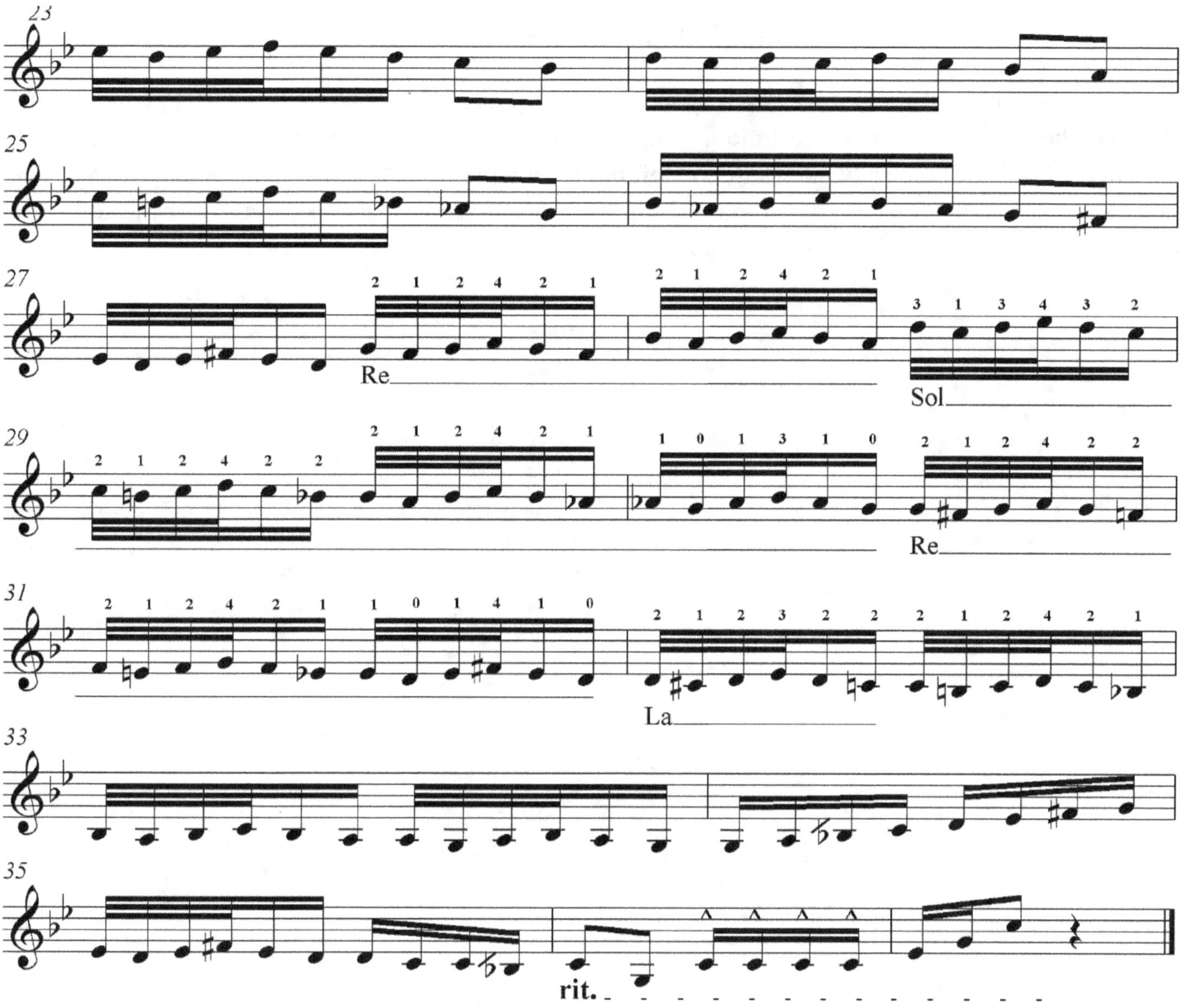

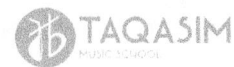

Qarar & Jawab Exercises

The two exercises below combine two important techniques of Oud playing: qarar and jawab, and fast risha strokes. Applying the two techniques together smoothly will greatly improve right hand technique, left hand dexterity and right and left hand coordination. As always, begin at a slower pace before gradually speeding up the tempo making sure to maintain tonal precision and the fluidity of movement.

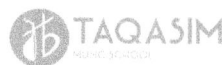

Exercise 1

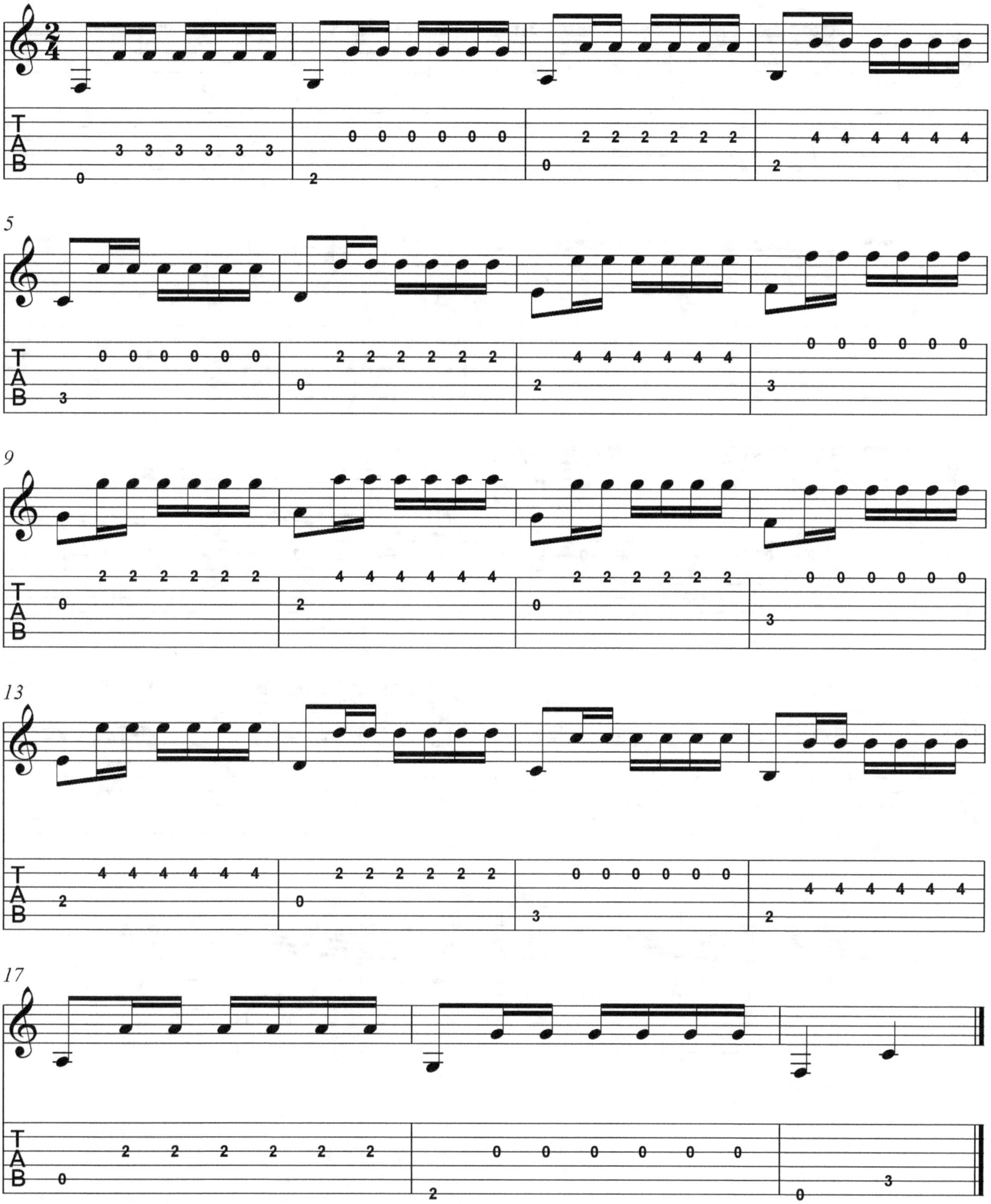

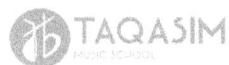

Exercise 2

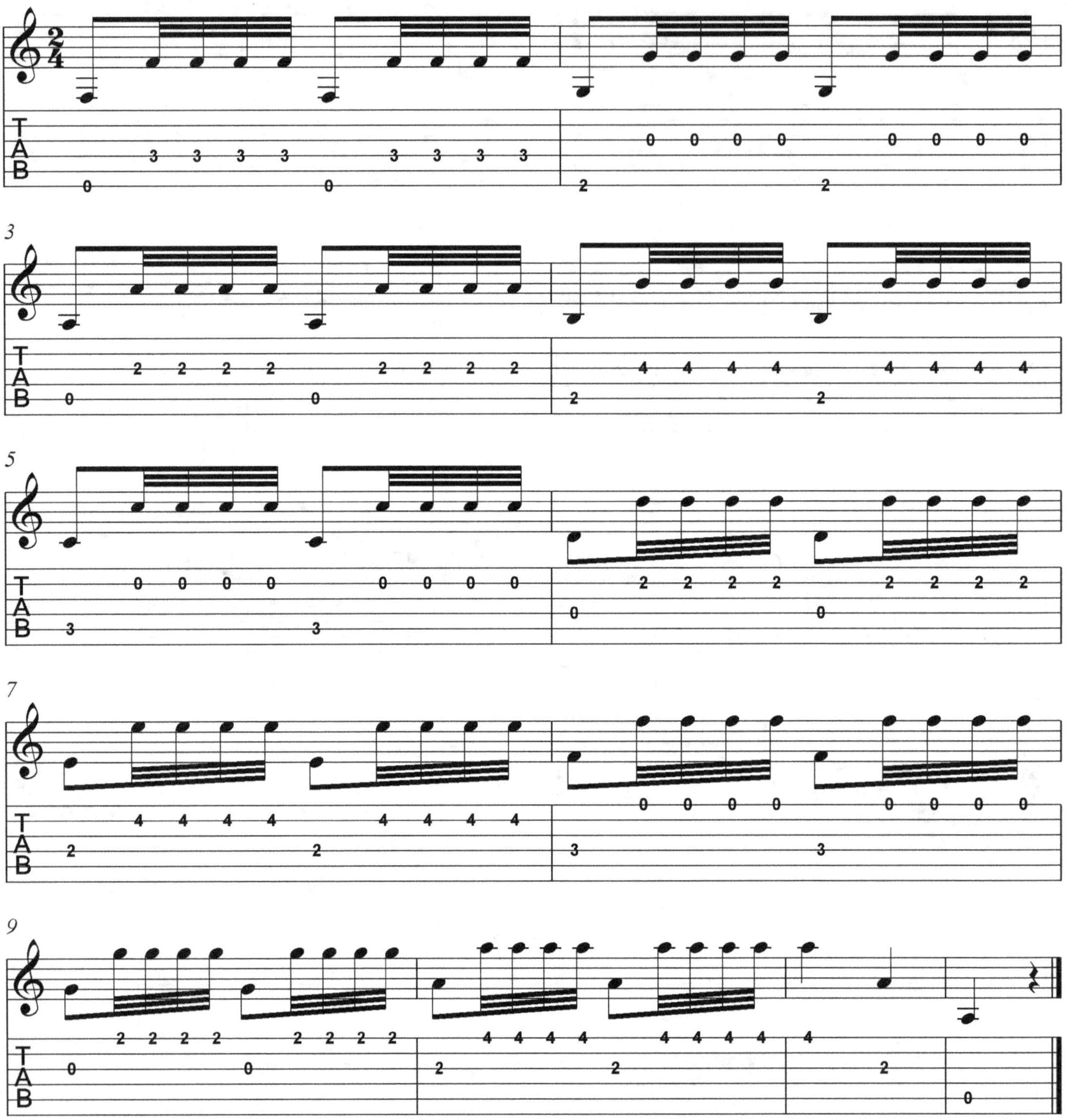

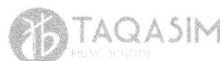

Samaa'i Nagriz – Royal Palace – A. Mukhtar

Royal Palace, is the introduction and *tasleem* to a piece written in *Maqam Negriz*. It was written using a complex rhythm of 9/8 time known as *Aqsaq*.

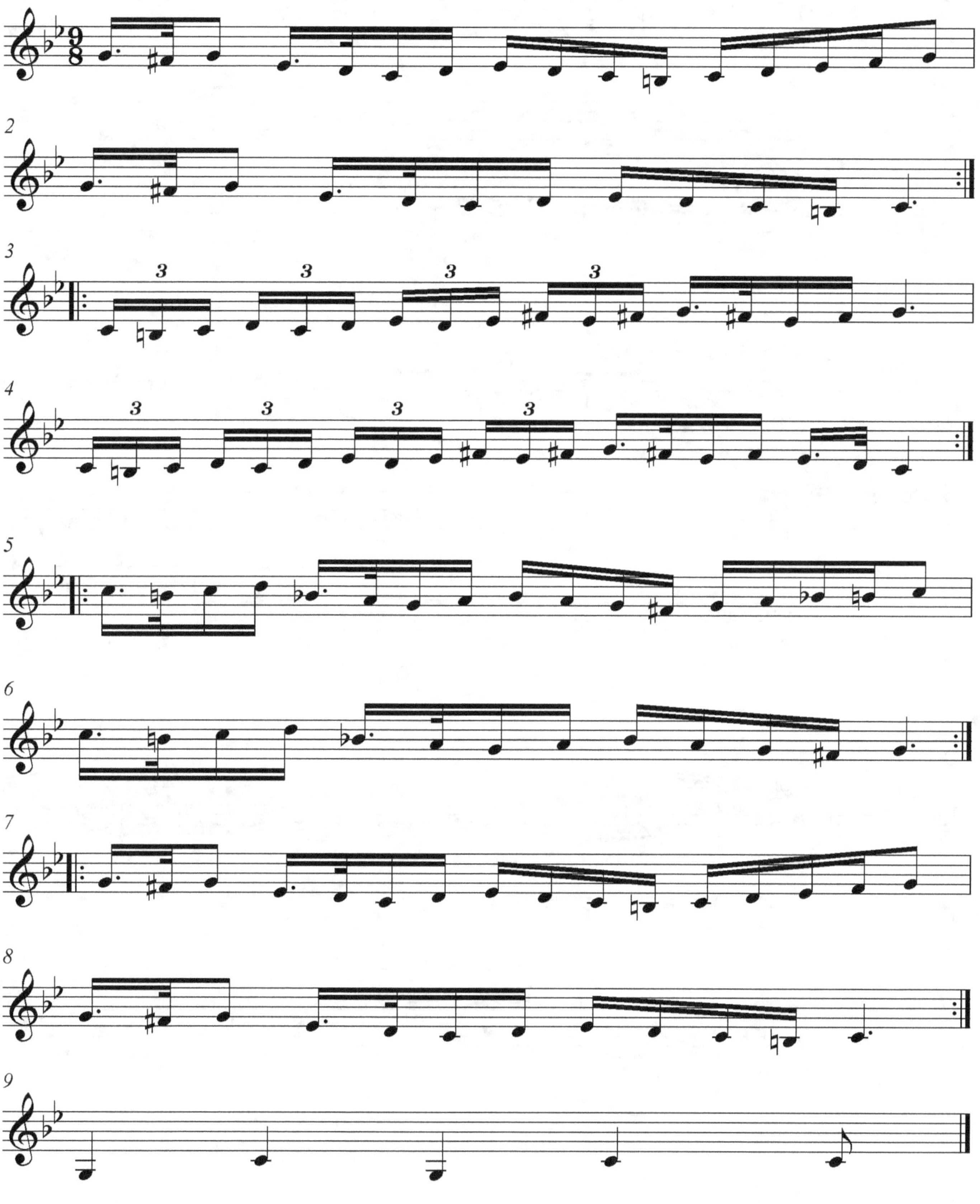

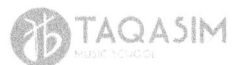

Samaa'i Nagriz – Darwish

This samaa'i was written by the composer Ali al-Darwish.

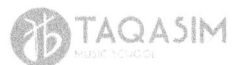

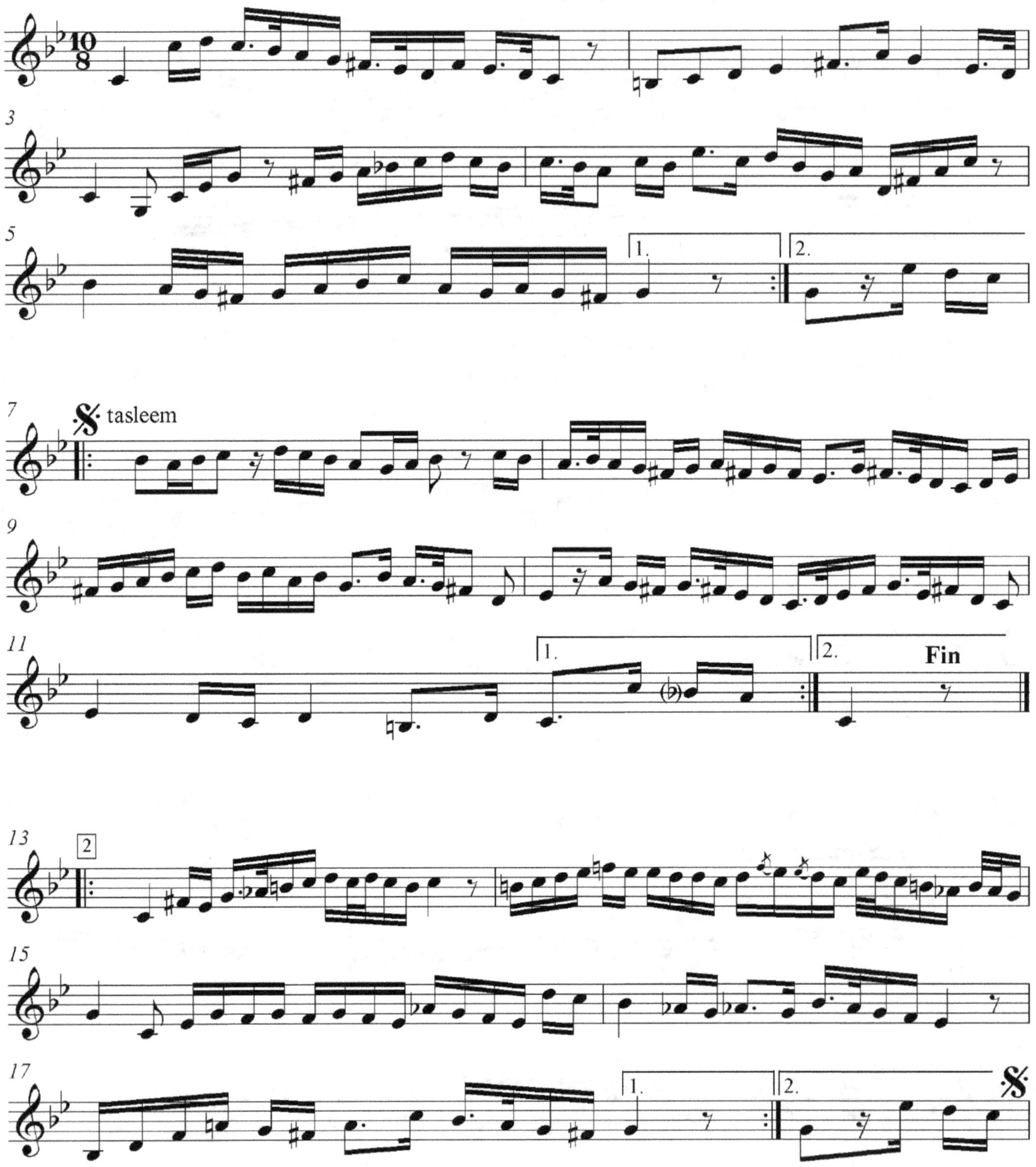

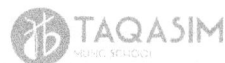

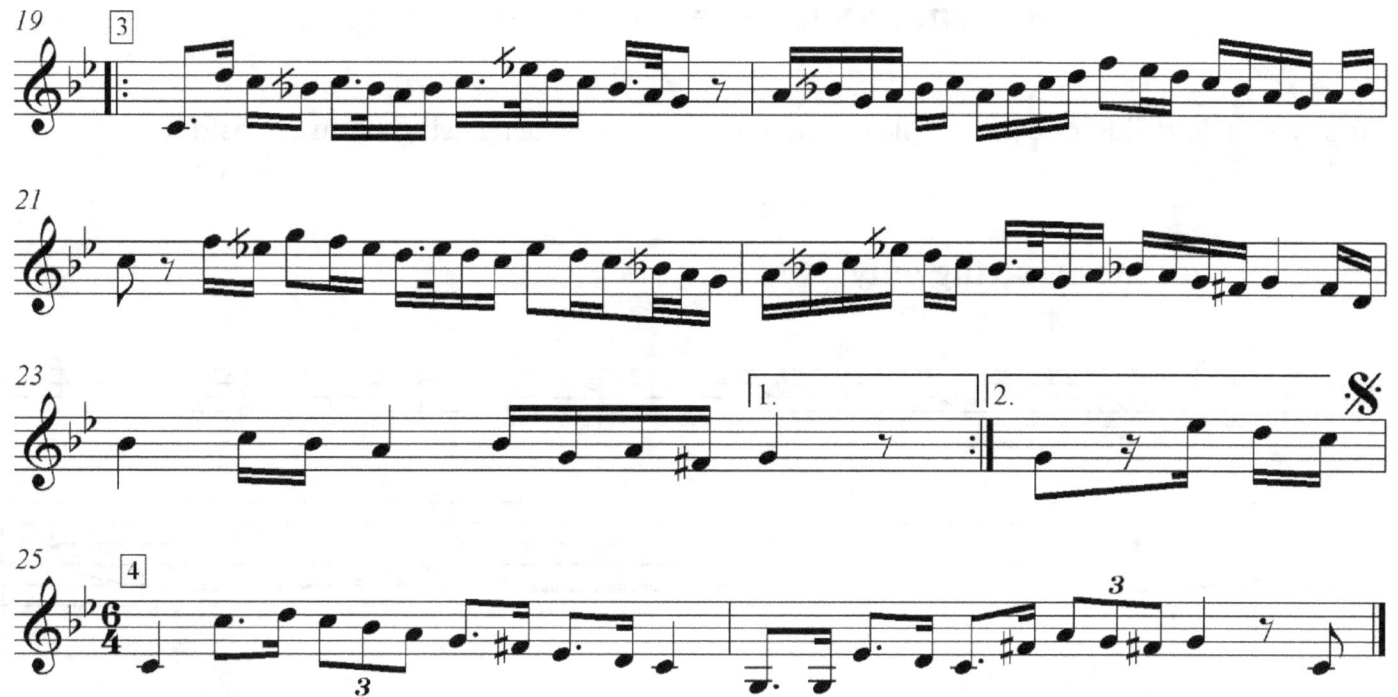

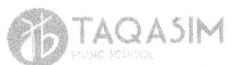

Maqam Bayat – Played on One String

The scores below illustrate how to play *Maqam Bayat* on one string using all three positions.

Bayat Sol – on the 4ᵗʰ string only

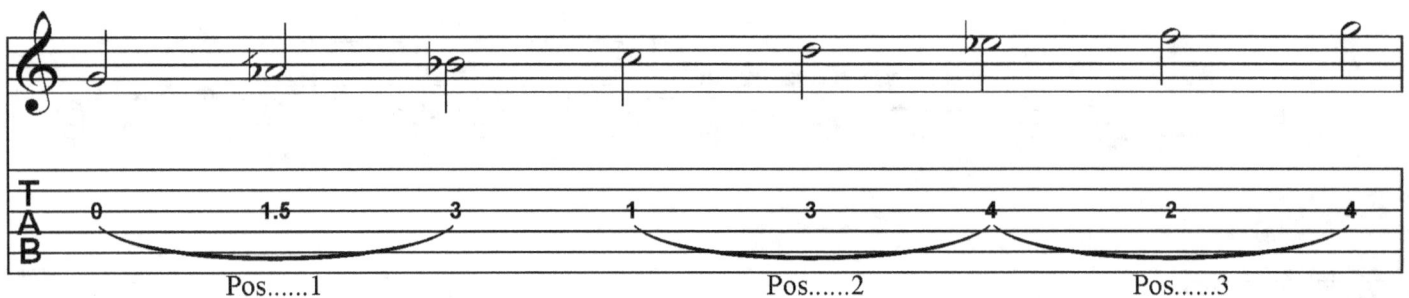

Bayat Re – on the 3ʳᵈ string only

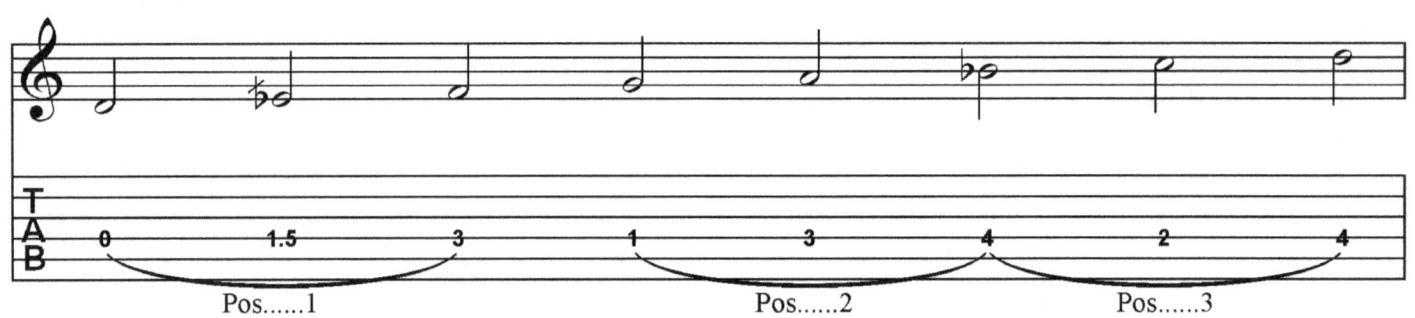

Bayat La – on the 2ⁿᵈ string only

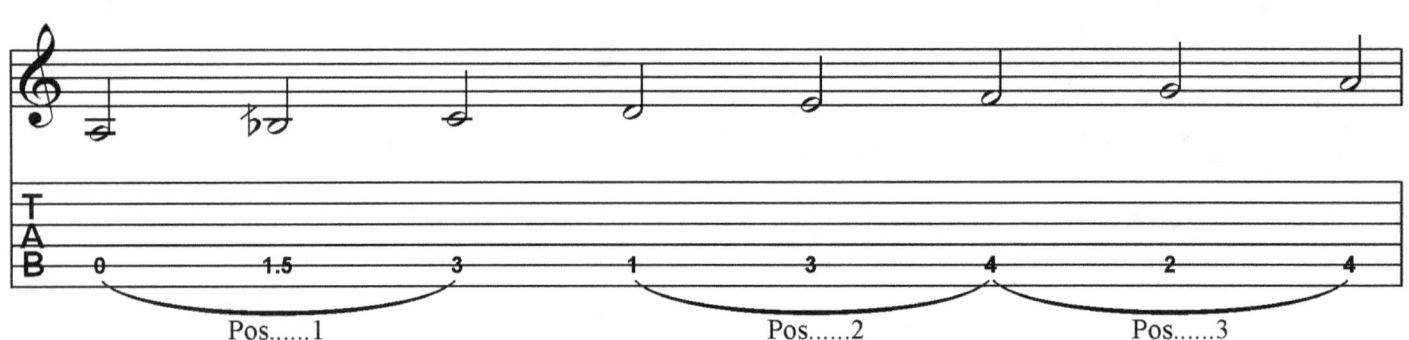

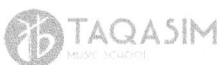

Sulaf – Bayat Re

This is a free-style composition, a masterpiece composed by *Ghanim Haddad.* A combination of *maqamaat* were used in the writing of this piece. Namely: *Rast, Bayat and Segah.* In order to execute this piece well, students must use consistent, clear and controlled down-up *risha* technique. The piece can be played at various speeds. However, correct fingering and tonal precision is essential at any speed. Begin slowly, gradually picking up speed while maintaining control of the notes being played.

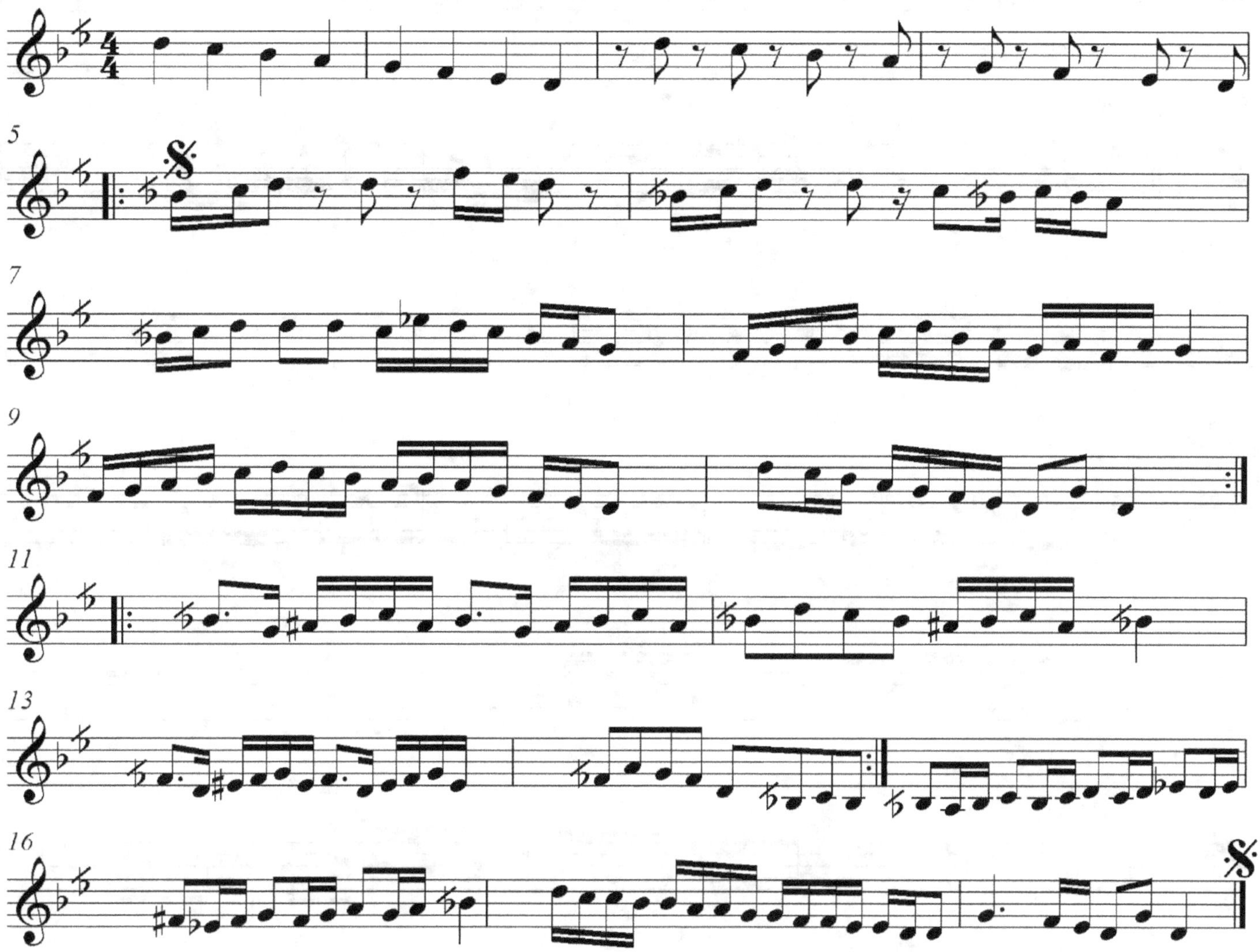

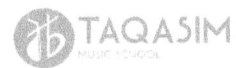

Sulaf – Bayat Sol

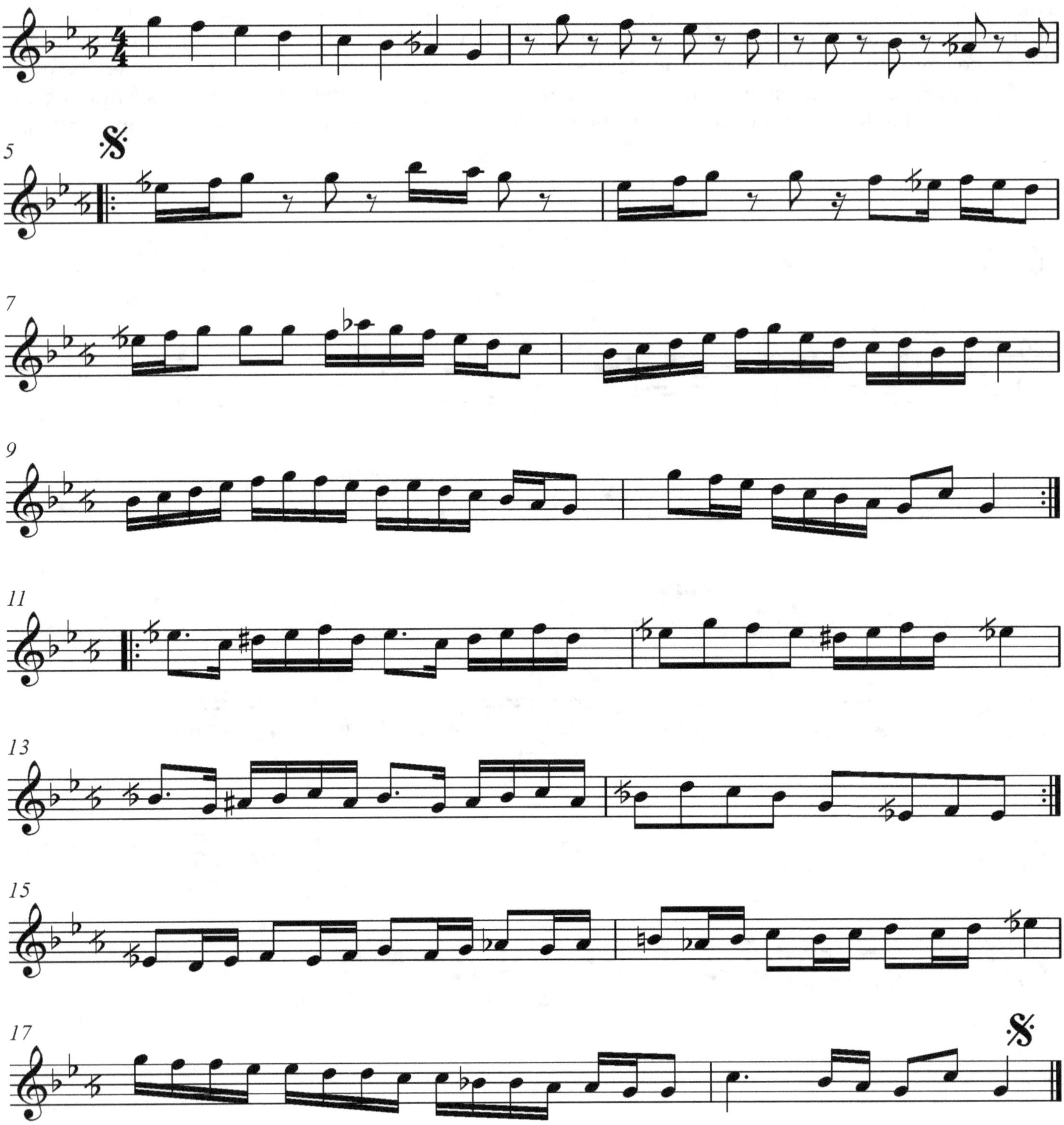

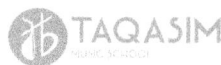

Maqam Saba

Below is a score representing *Maqam Saba* Re in two octaves using the first, second and third left-hand positions.

Saba Re – 2 octaves

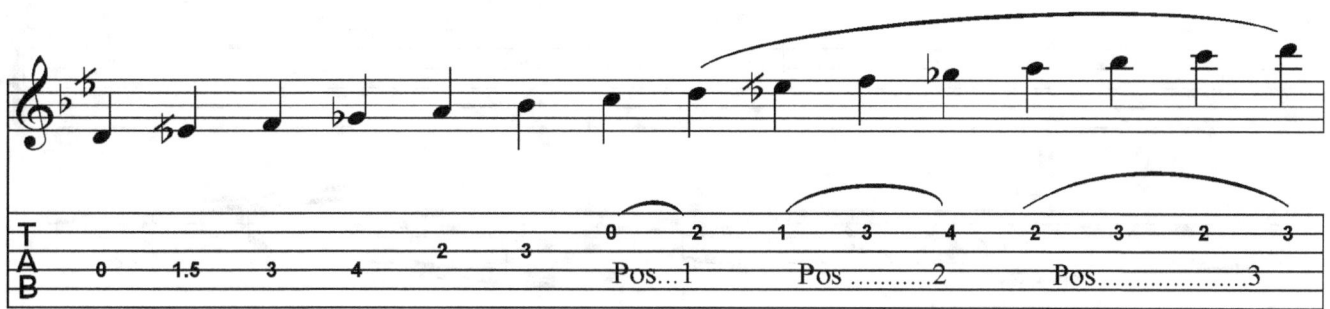

Doulab Saba Re 1

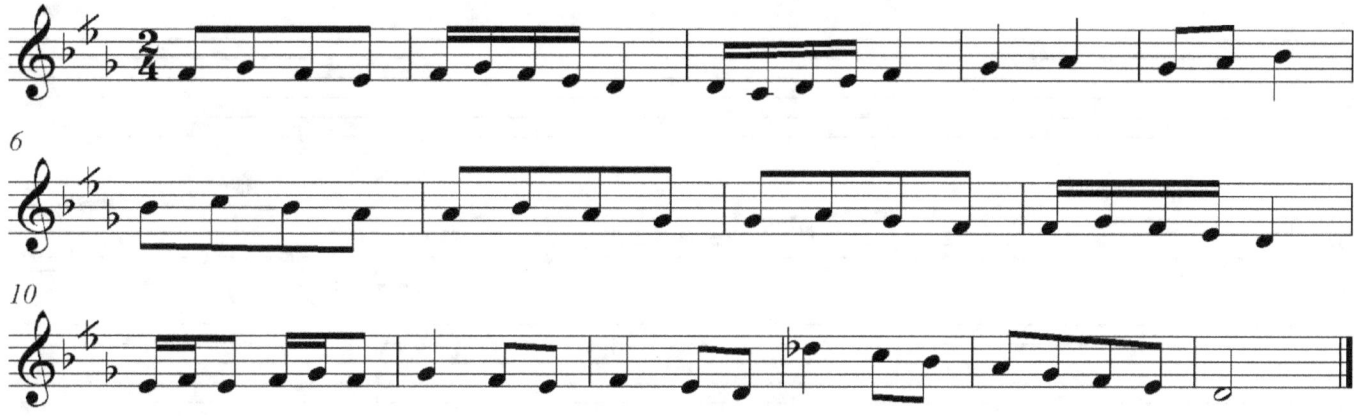

Doulab Saba Re 2

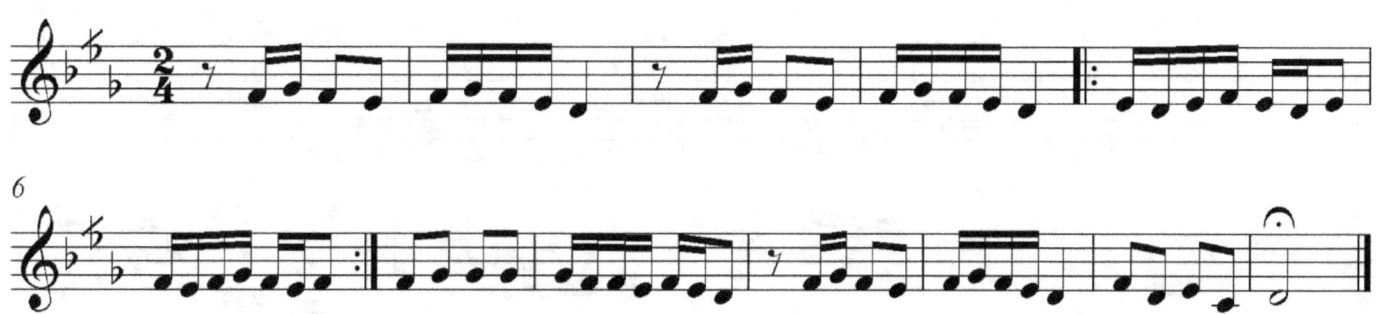

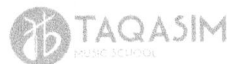

Etude Saba Re

This etude is designed it further develop *risha* technique and speed of execution along with practicing to play in the second octave in *Maqam Saba*.

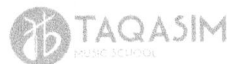

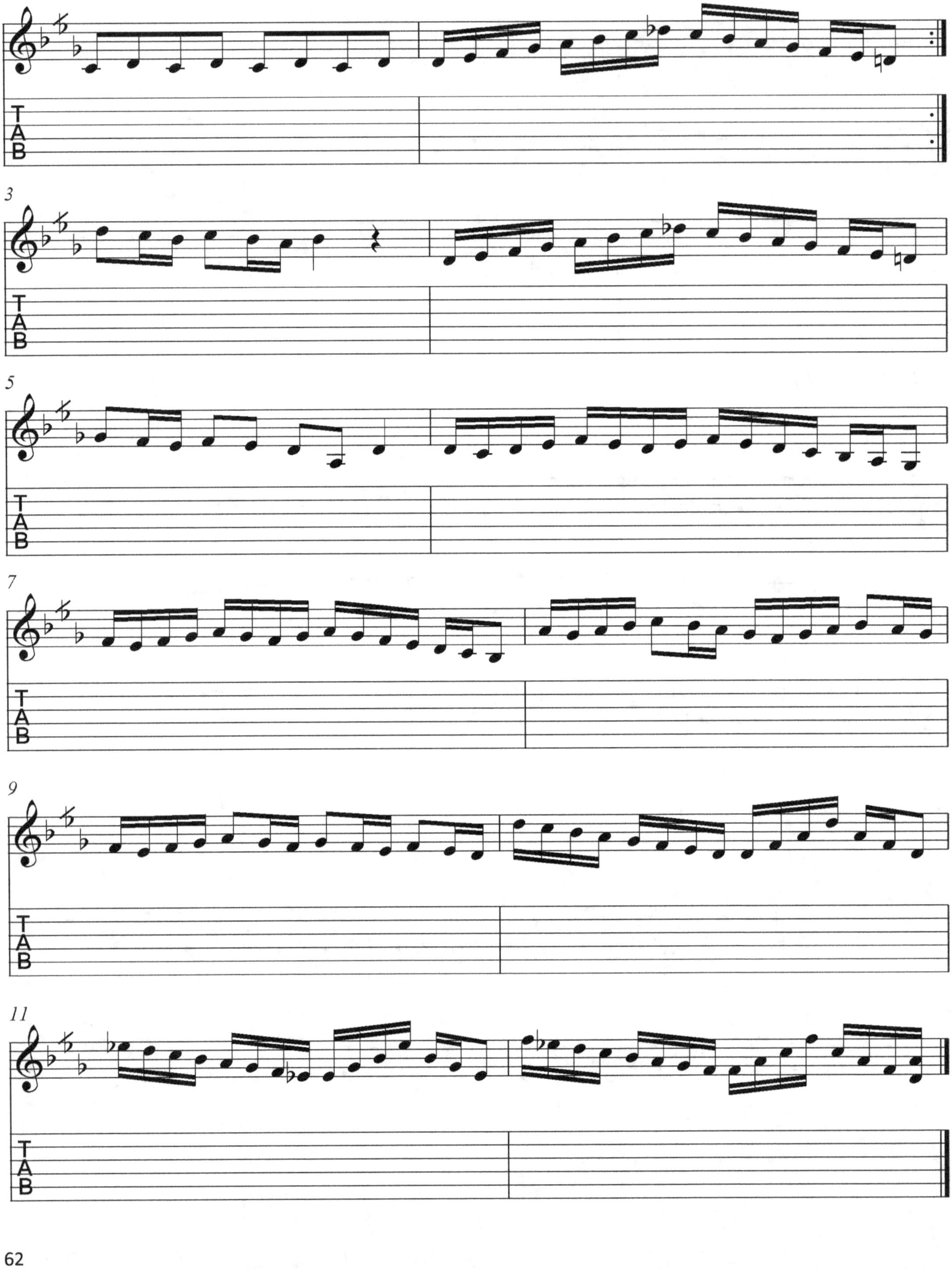

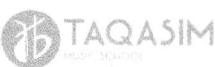

Trills

Remember that a *trill/zaghrada* is achieved by playing one note of a *maqam* and tapping the next note up. The first note is struck by the *risha,* while the second is only tapped on the finger-board without the use of the *risha*. This exercise is written in *Maqam Ajam* but the concept can be applied to any *maqam* scale.

In the score below, the trilled notes are written in brackets ( ) and have the letters "tr" written above them.

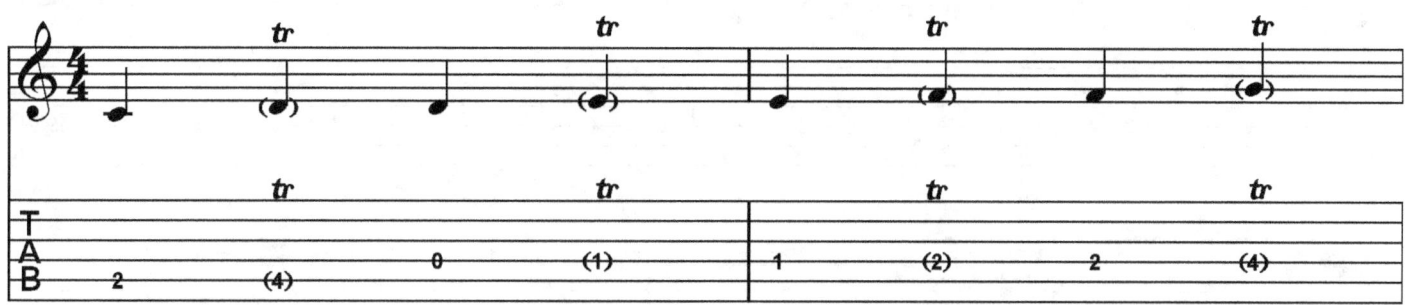

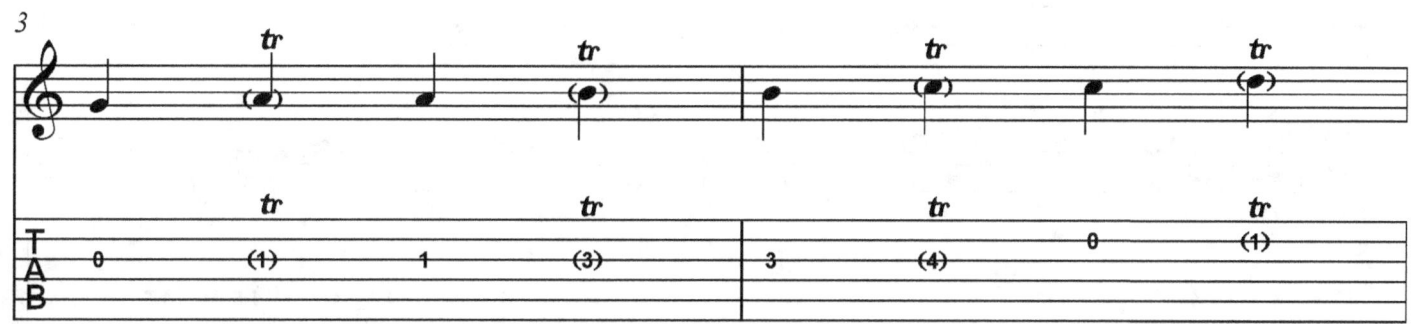

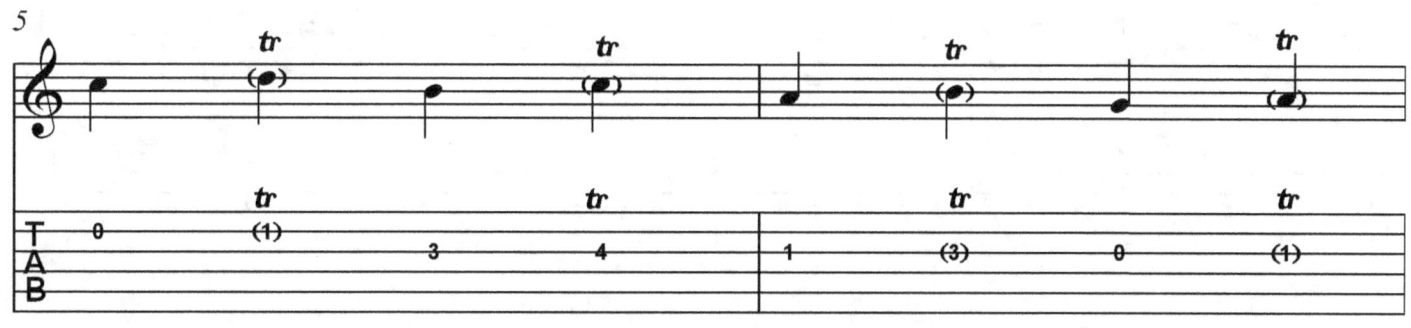

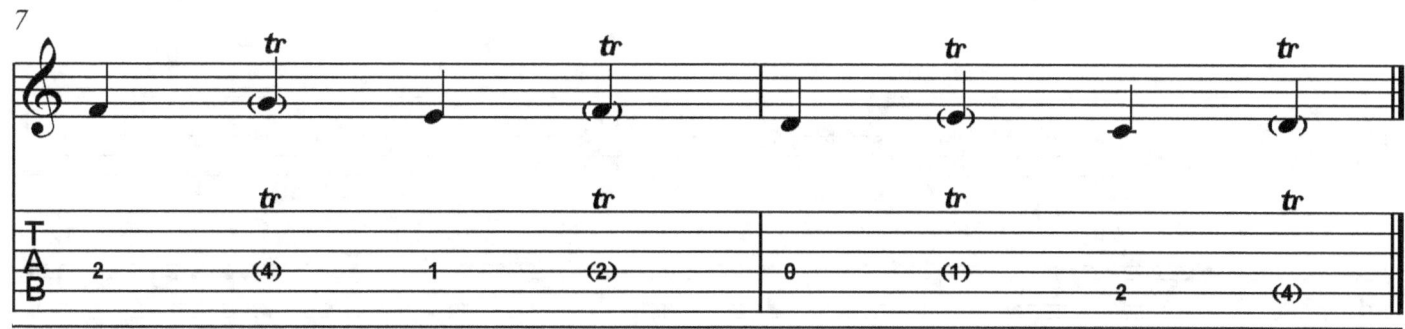

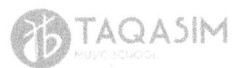

Samaa'i Saba

This samaa'i, written by *Iskander Nano*, although note very technical, is a very good representation of *Maqam Saba's* spirit.

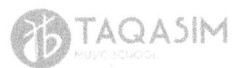

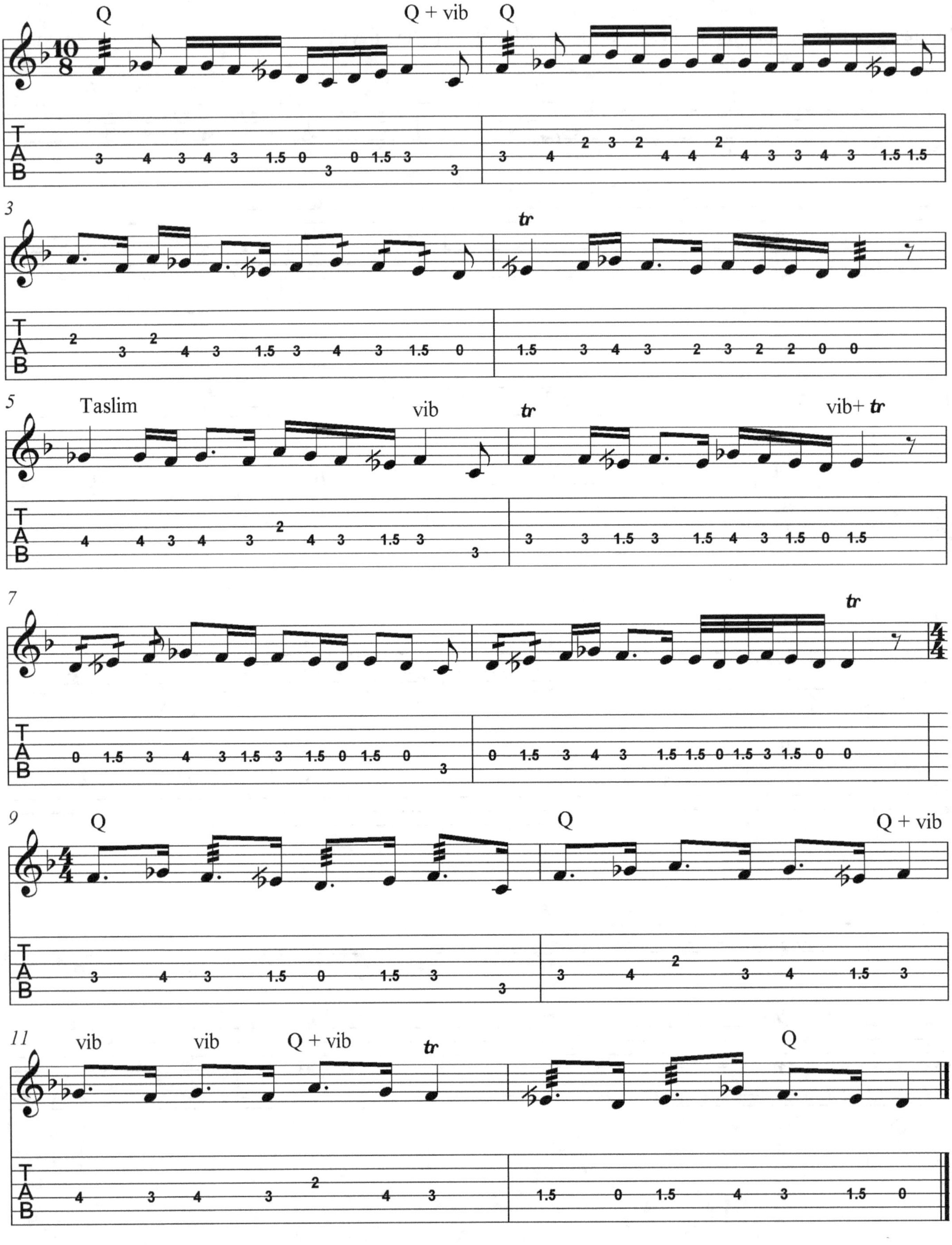

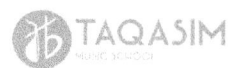

Samaa'i Saba – Khaled Mohamad Ali

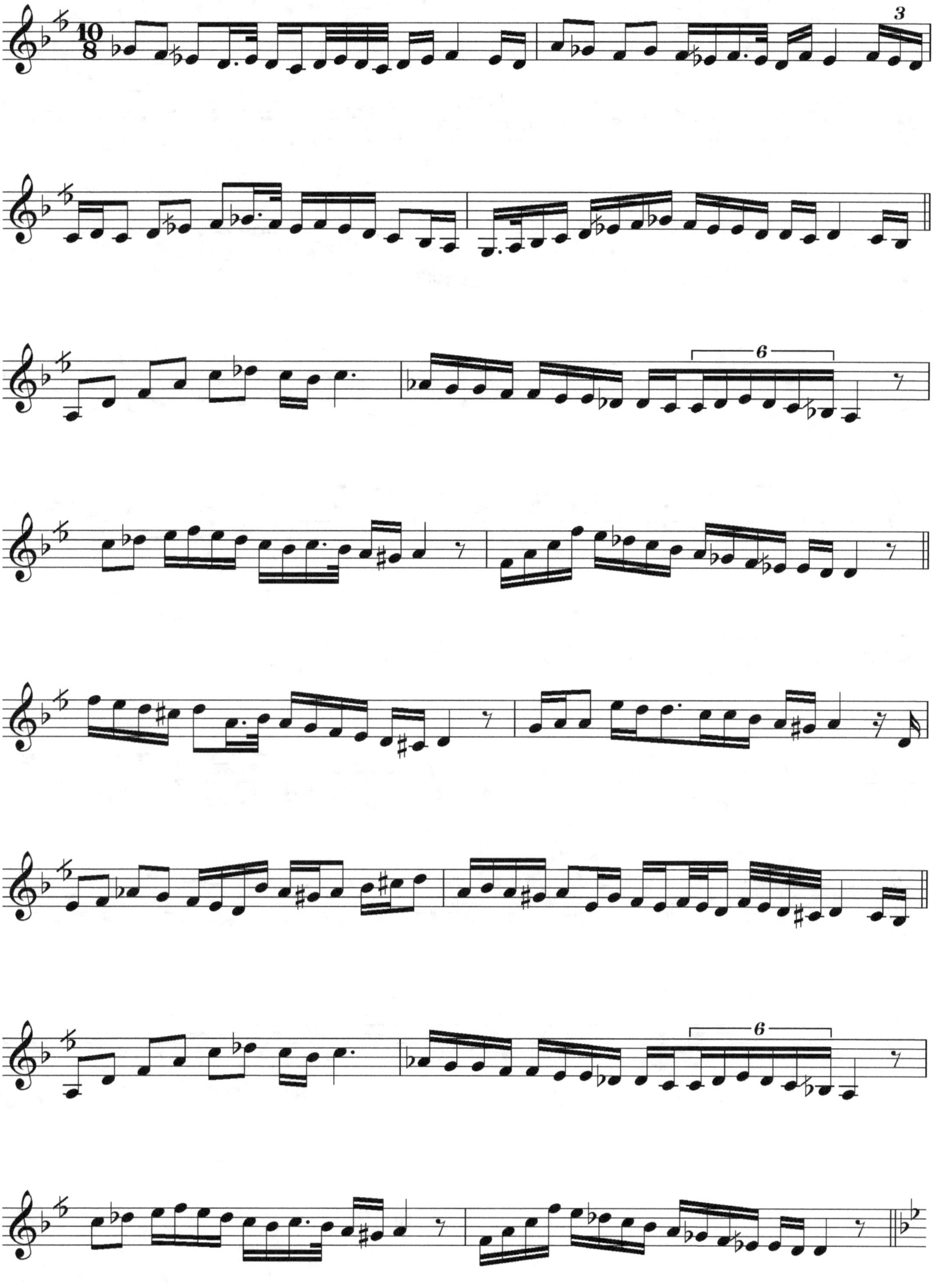

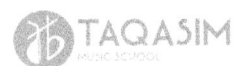

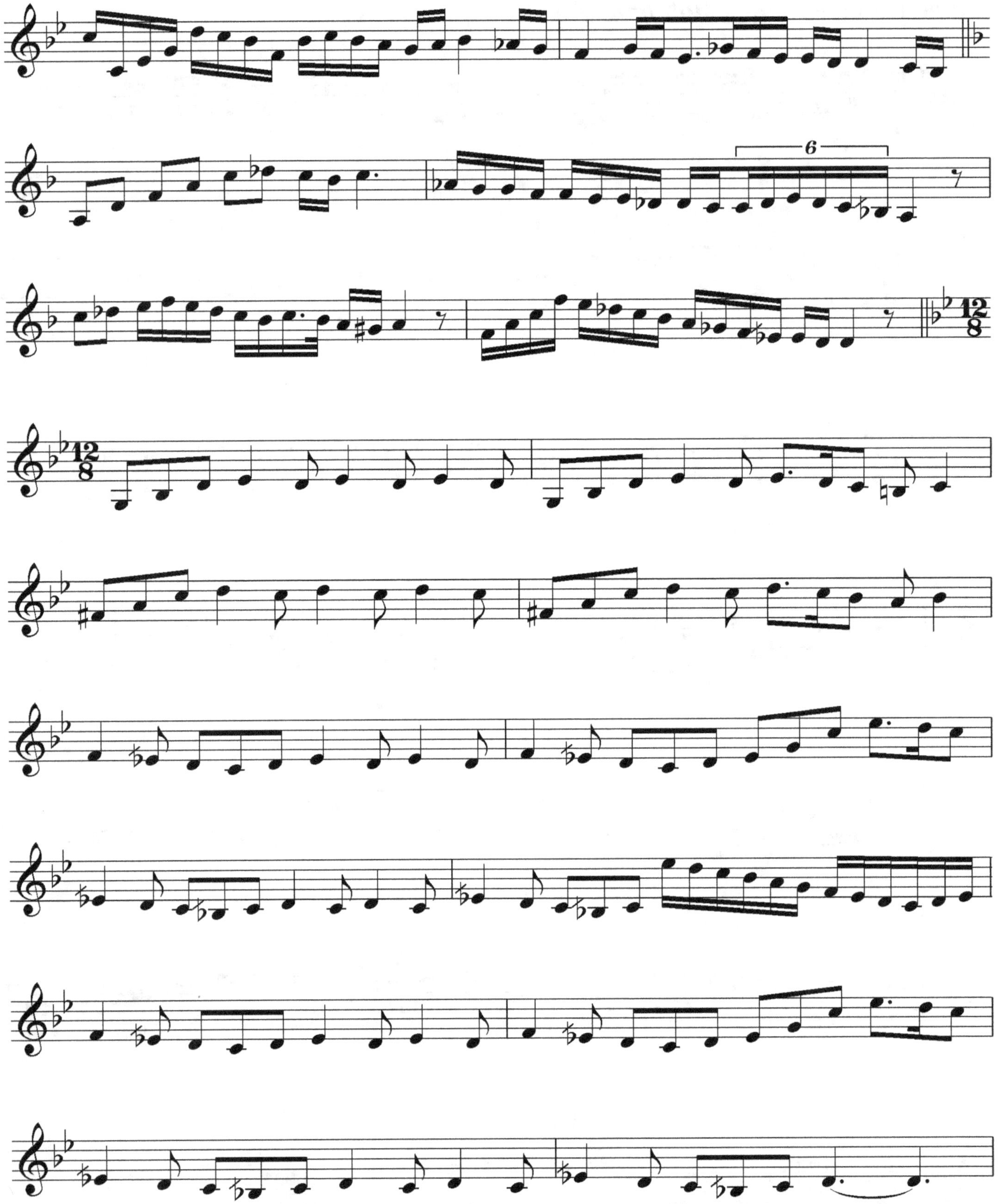

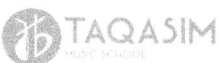

Huwa Sahih el-Hawa Ghallab

Huwa Sahih el-Hawa Ghallab was written in *Maqam Saba* Re and sung by Umm Kulthoum.
It is advised to begin by playing the introduction to the song which ends in bar 13. Once mastered, move on to tackle the rest of the song. The numbers 1 and 2 in the score show that the musician can play the rest note the first time the measure is played and the eighth-note when the measure is repeated.

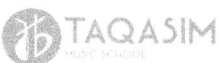

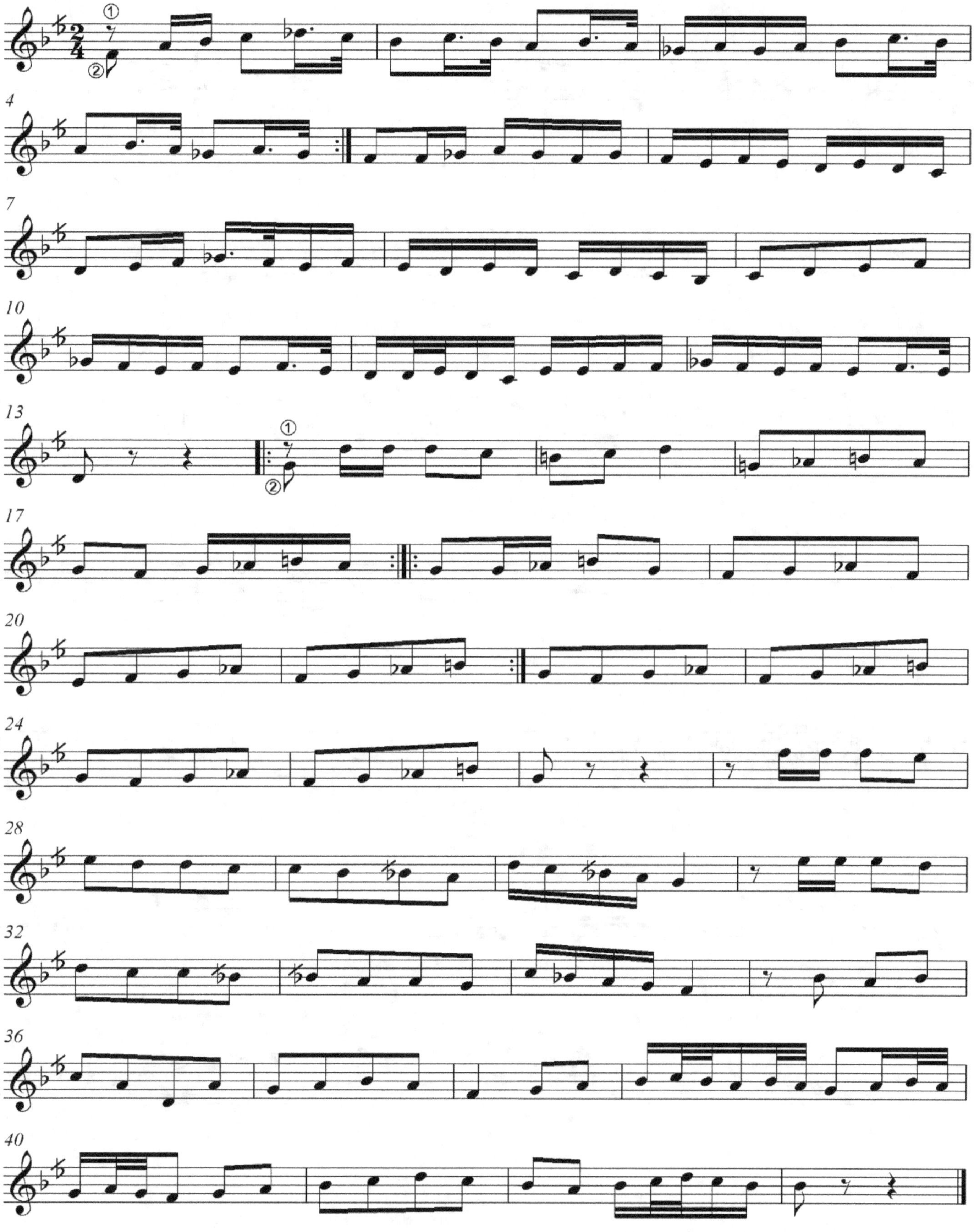

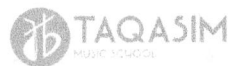

Blues Saba Sol – A. Mukhtar

This piece is considered to be a free-style composition. Notice the double notes in measures 22 and 23. These notes are meant to be strummed rather than picked.

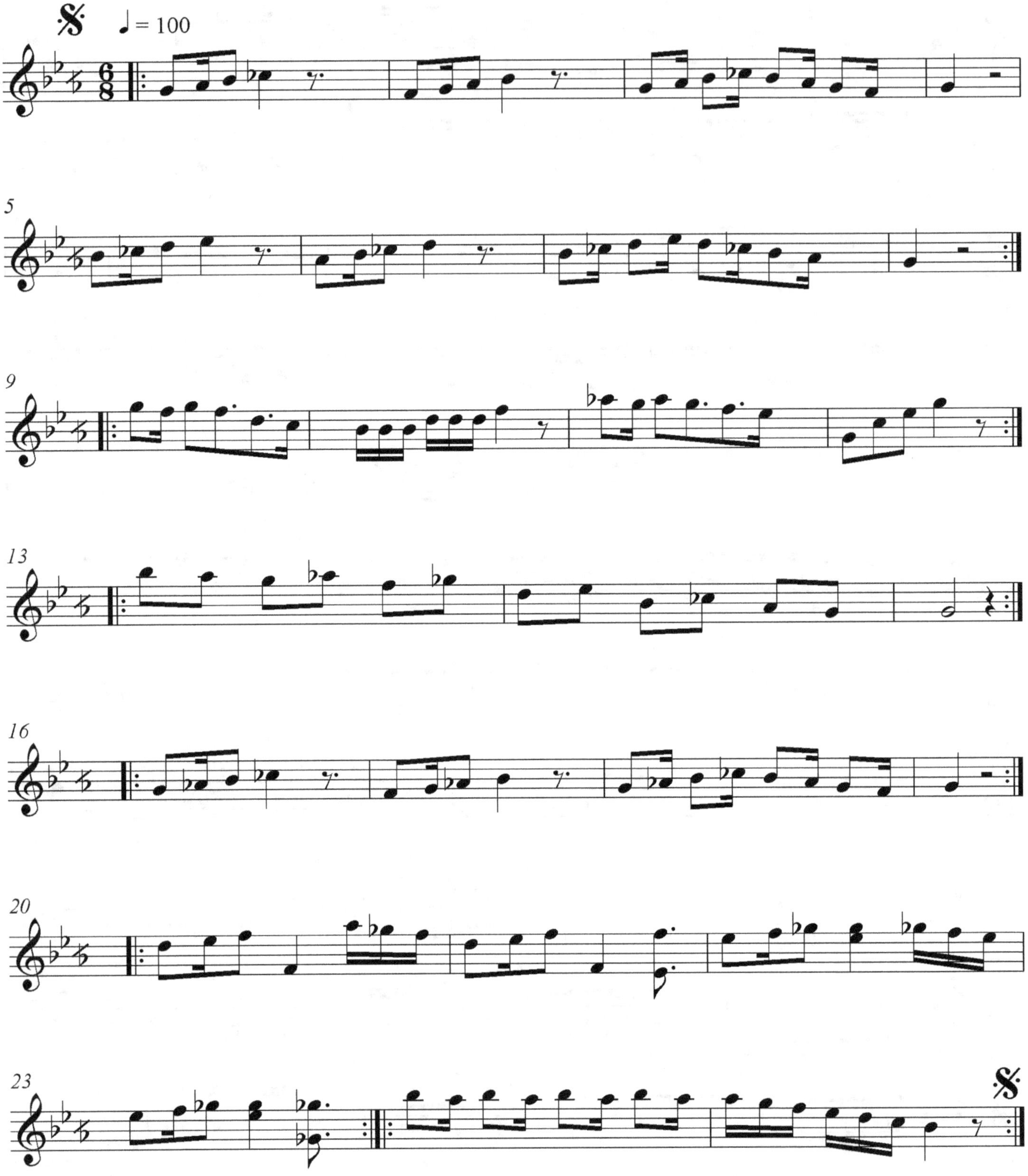

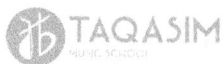

Maqam Segah

Below is a score representing *Maqam Segah* Mi half-flat in two octaves using the first and second left-hand positions. Be sure to play Mi half-flat very accurately as it is the settled note in this *maqam* and sets tone for the coming intervals.

Segah Mi half-flat – 2 octaves

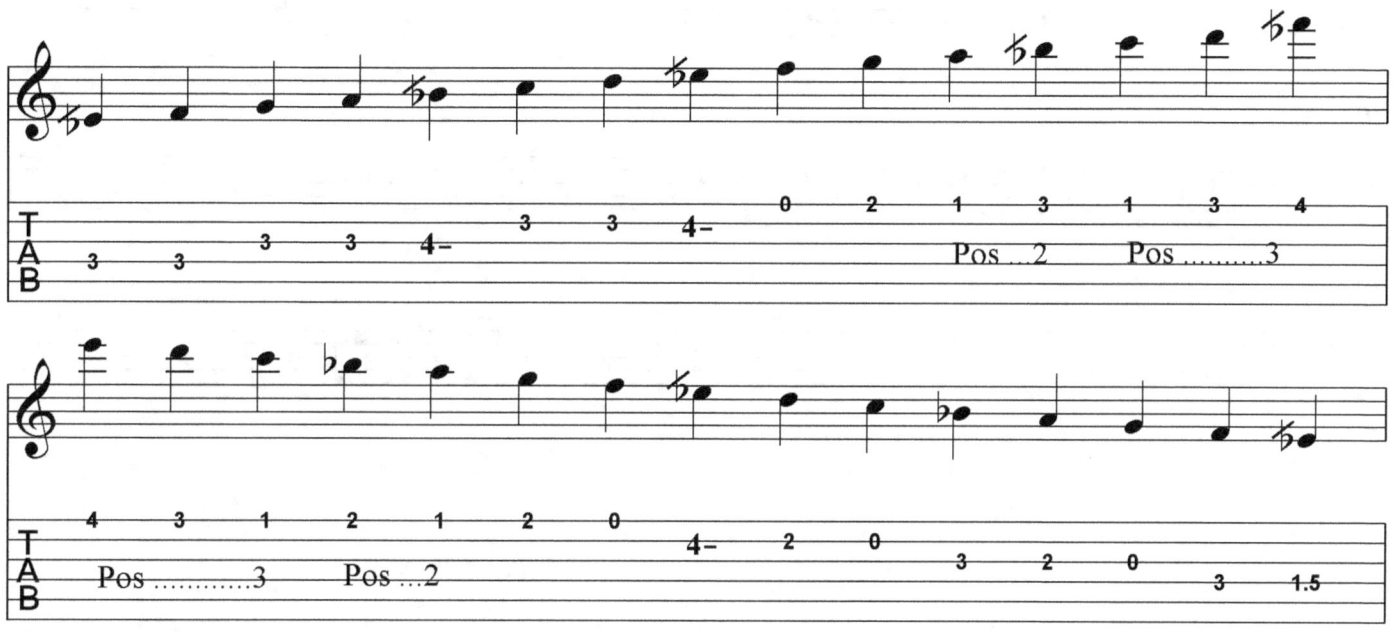

Doulab Segah Mi half-flat 1

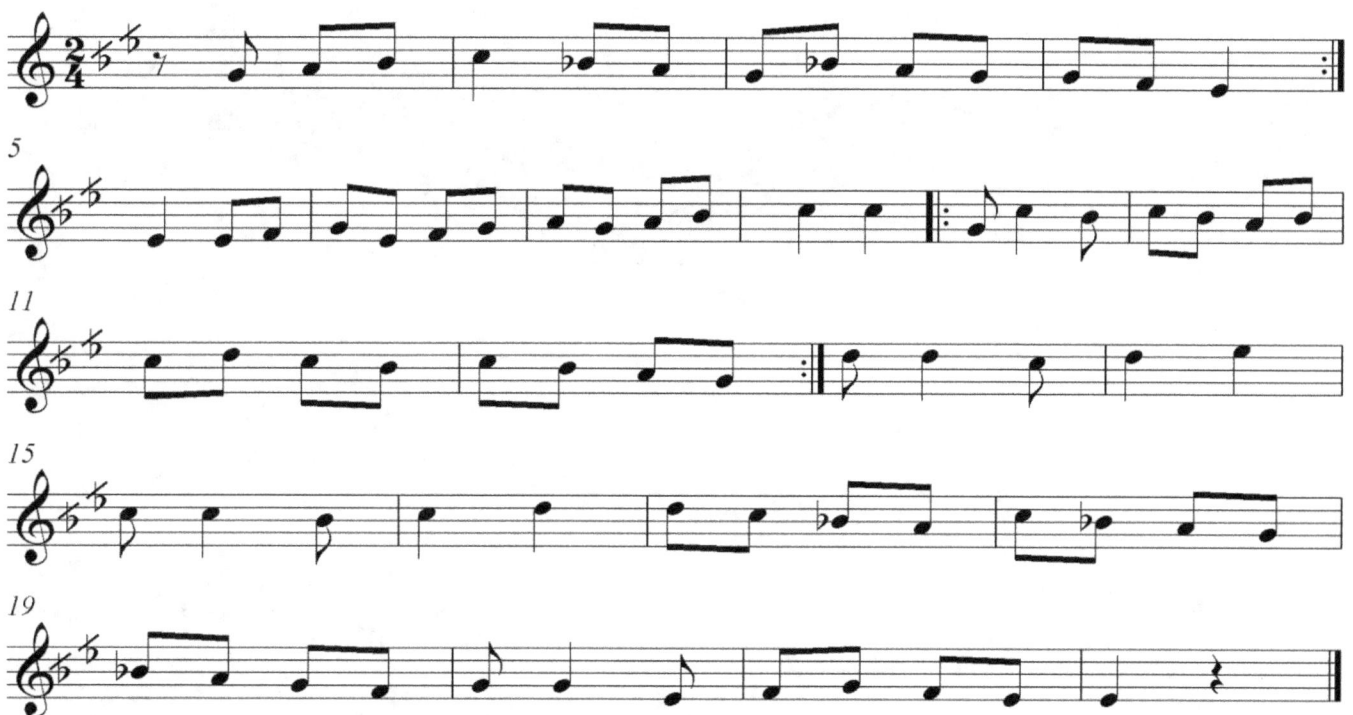

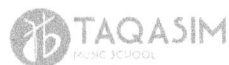

Doulab Segah Mi half-flat 2

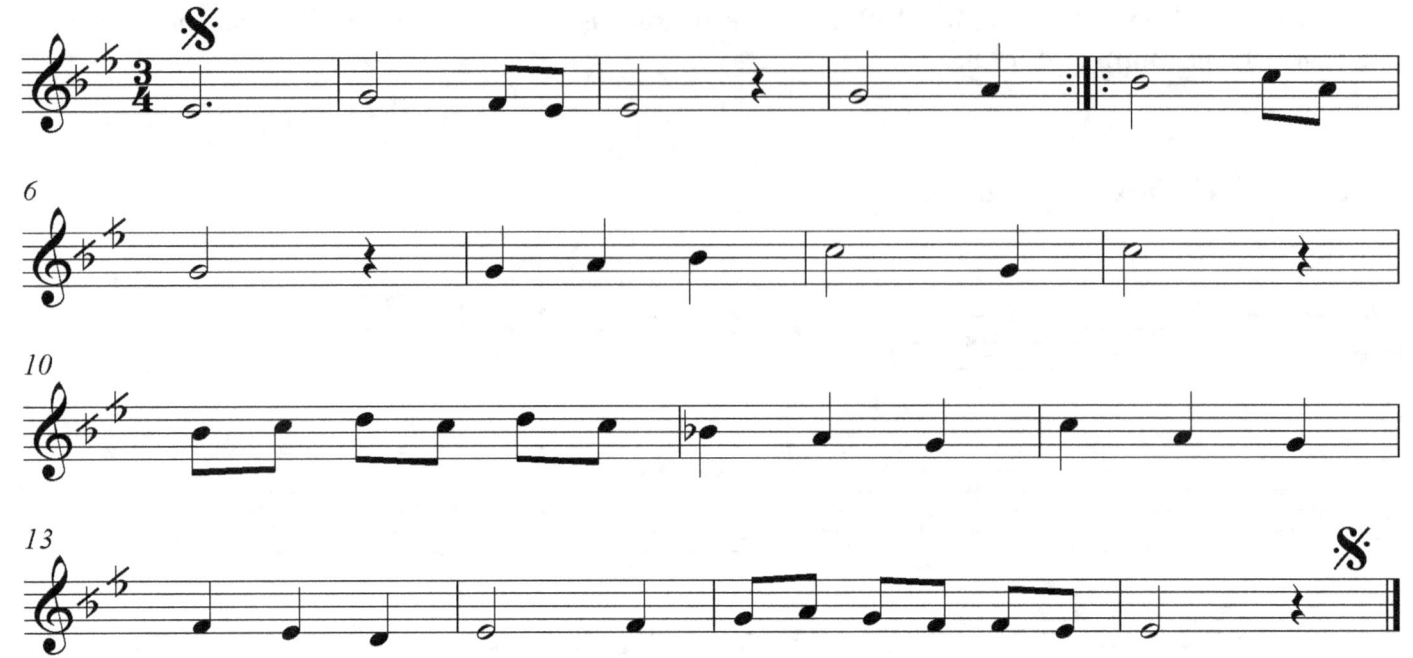

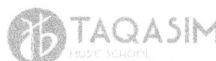

Etude Maqam Segah

This etude is good practice for fast *risha* technique.

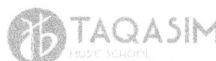

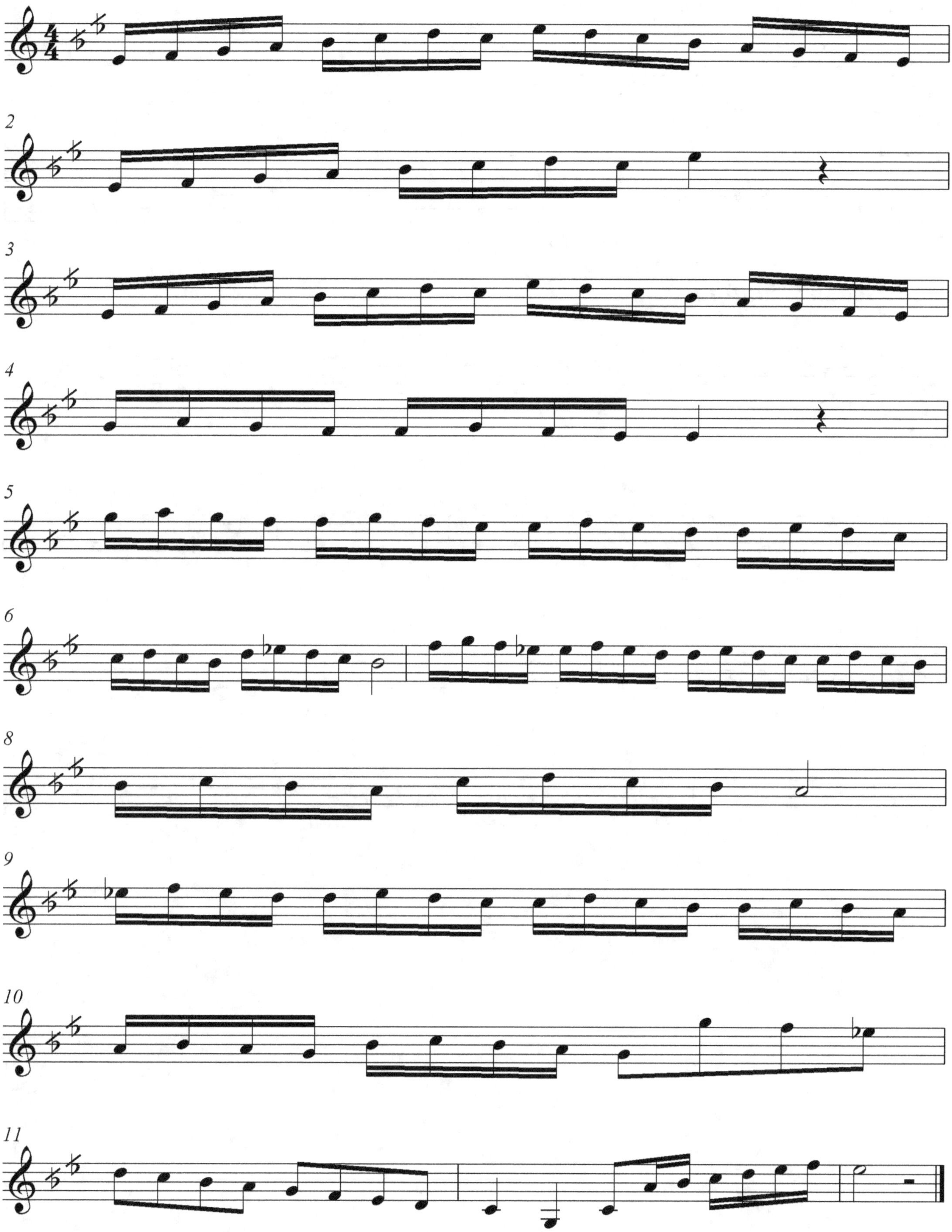

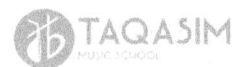

Maqam Segah Si half-flat

Below is a representation of *Maqam Segah* transposed to Si half-flat. The second octave has not been written. Try to play the second octave on your own.

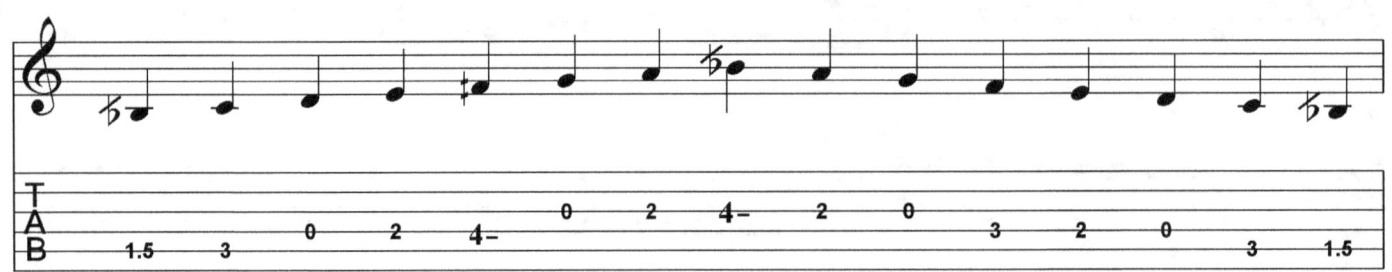

Etude Segah Si half-flat

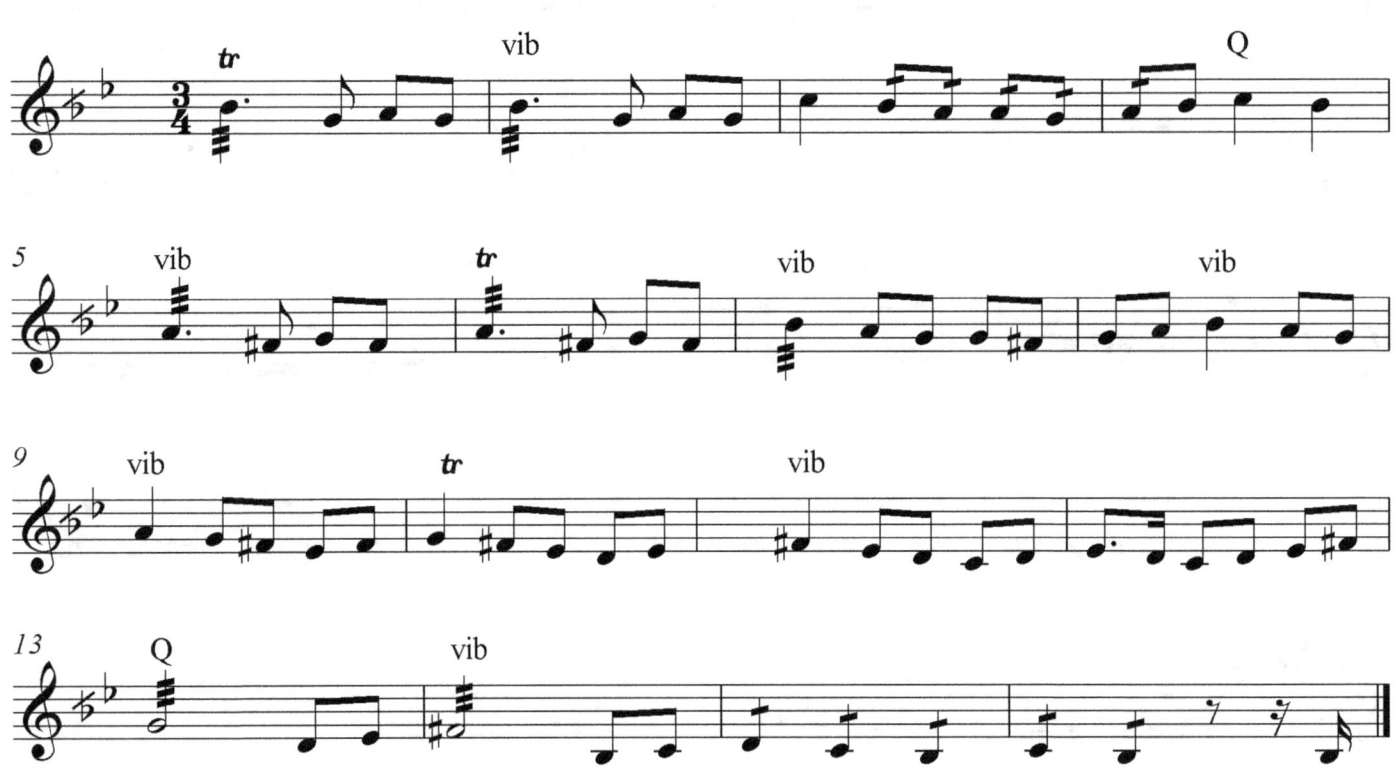

72

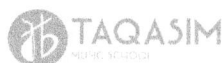

Samba Segah

This is a free-style piece that uses a lot of triplets and doubled notes.

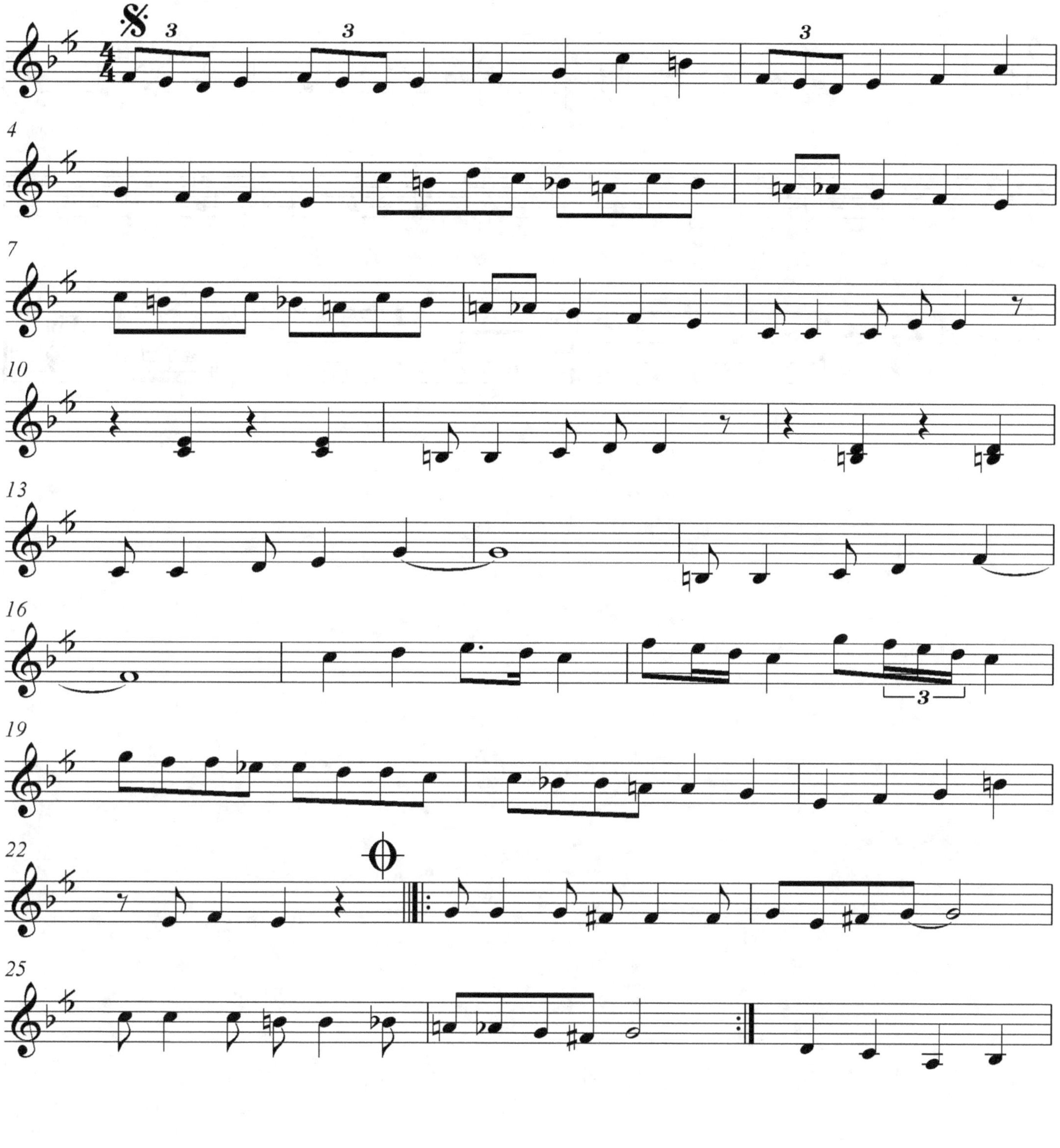

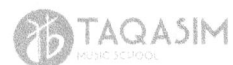

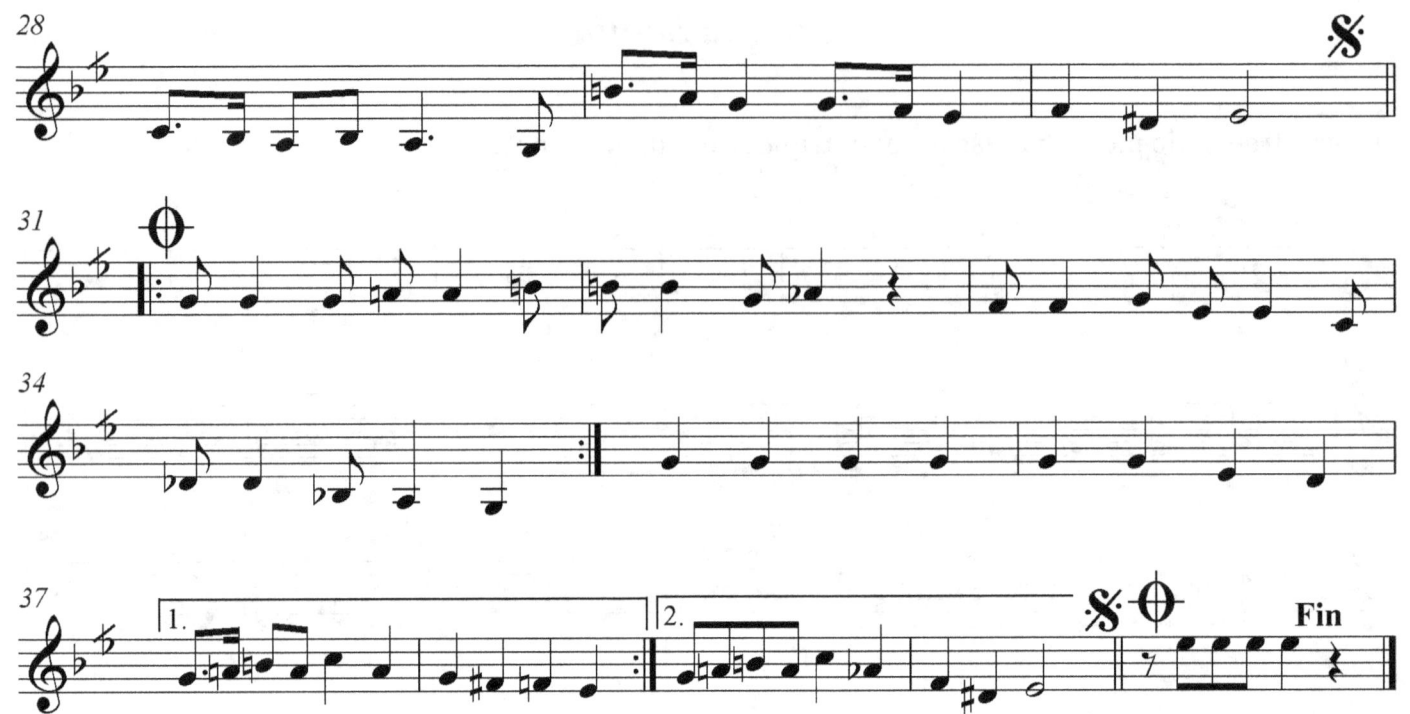

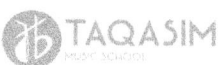

Maqam Huzam

Maqam Huzam is a secondary maqam from *Segah* as the first tetrachord shares the same interval. Below is a score illustrating *Maqam Huzam* Mi half-flat in two octaves, using two left-hand positions.

Huzam Mi half-flat

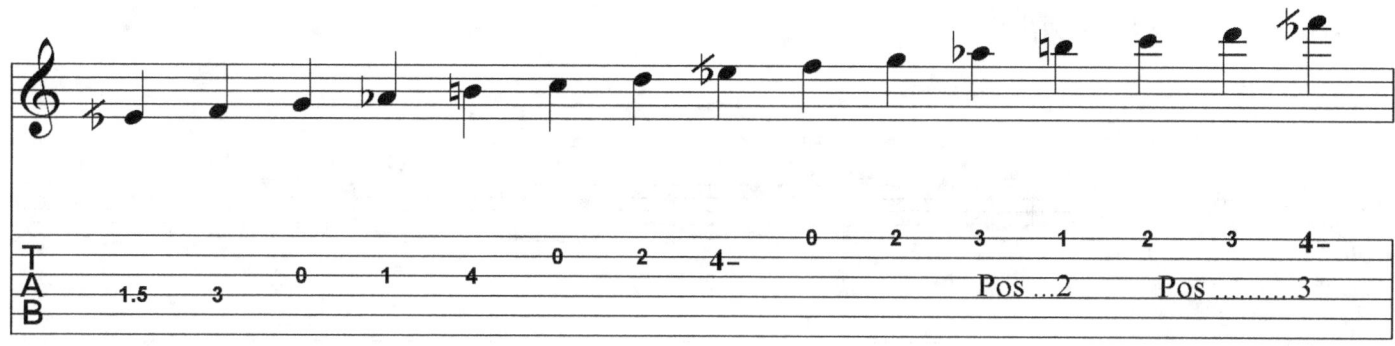

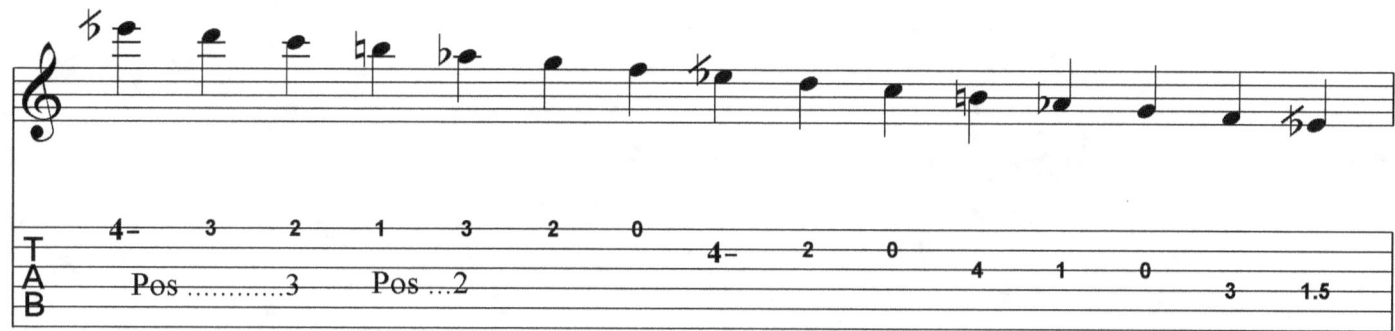

Doulab Huzam Mi half-flat

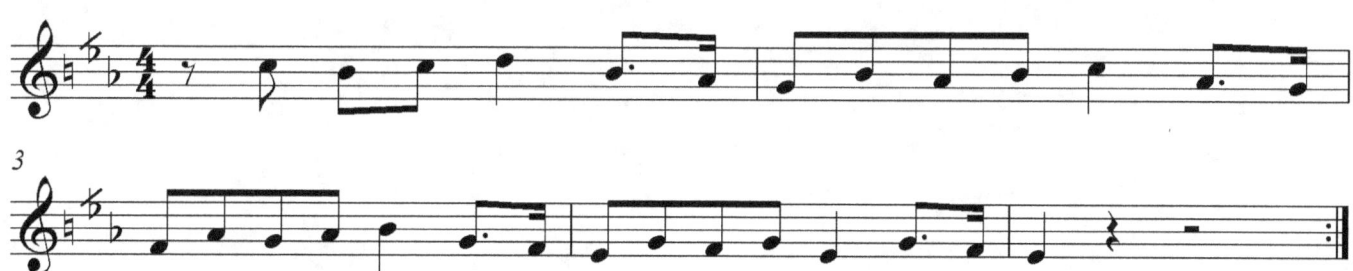

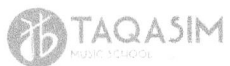

Maqam Huzam La half-flat

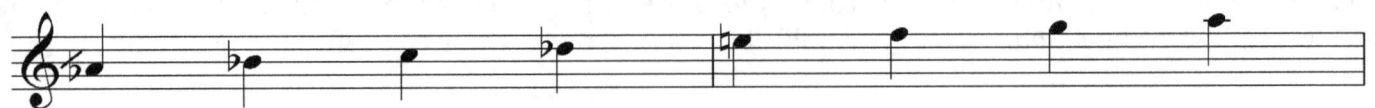

Doulab Huzam La half-flat

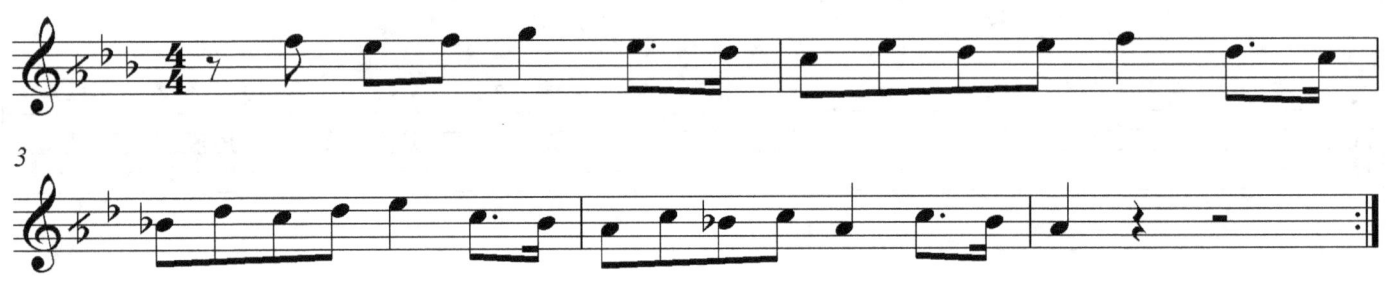

76

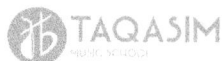

Etude Huzam Mi – Motez Salih

This etude in Maqam Huzam was written by Motez M. Salih.

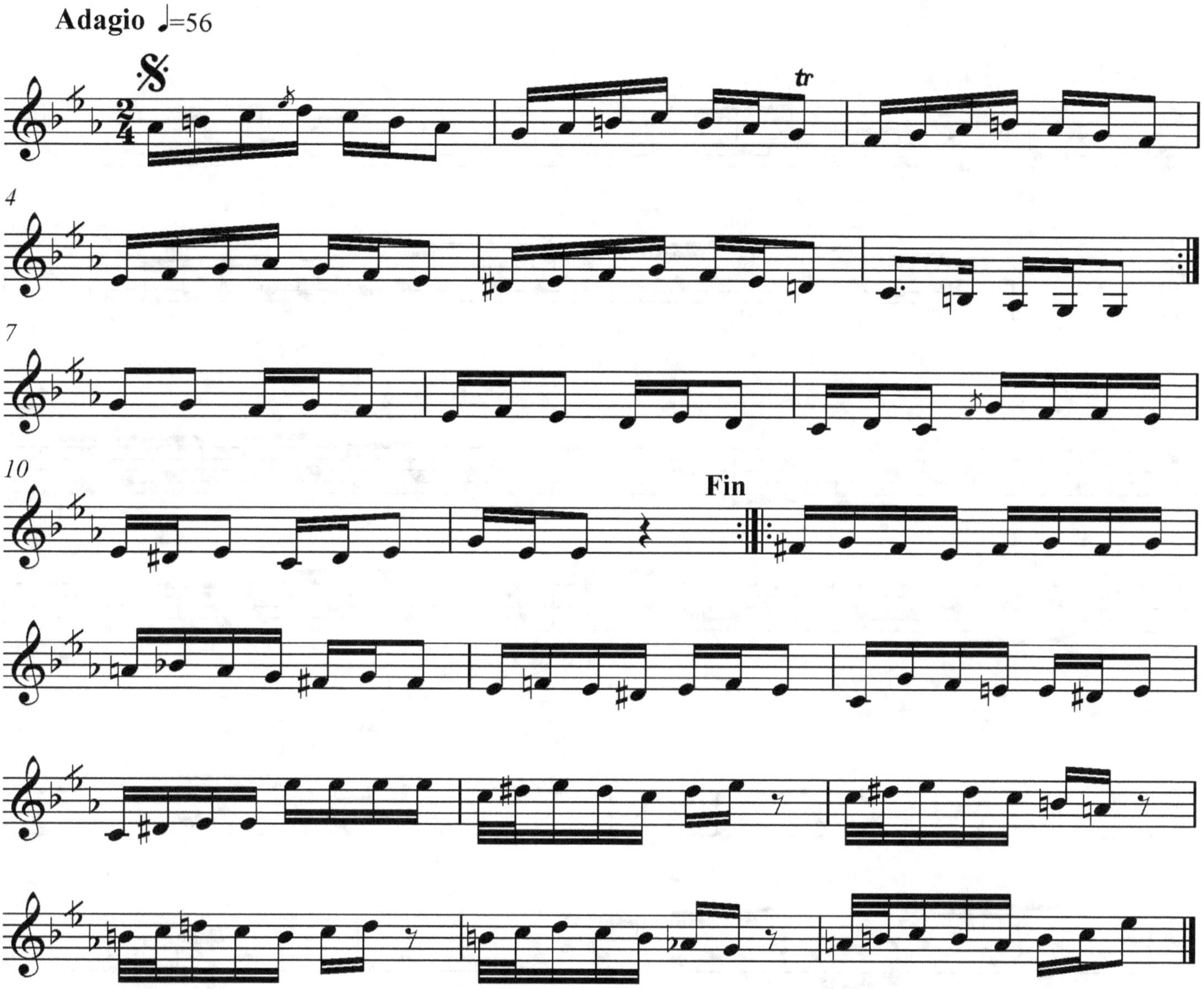

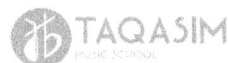

Samaa'i Huzam – Sherif M. Haider

The score below is the first *khanah* and the *taslim* of a *samaa'i* written in *Maqam Huzam* by Sherif M. Haider.

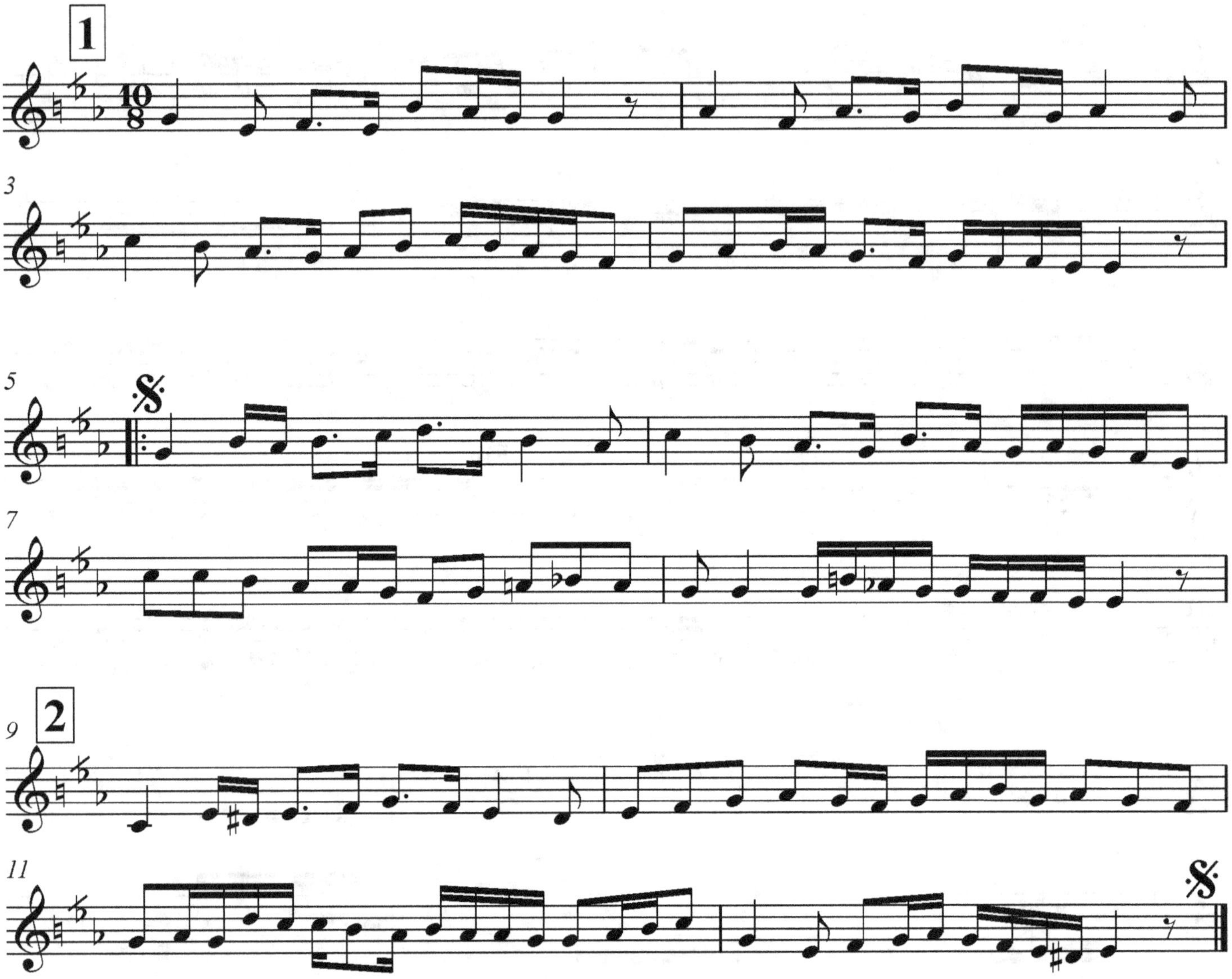

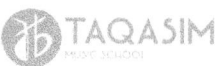

Al-Ward Gamil

The below score is an introduction to a song that was written in the 1920's by the Egyptian composer Zakariyya Ahmed using Maqam Huzam Si half-flat. It was sung by many Egyptian singers.

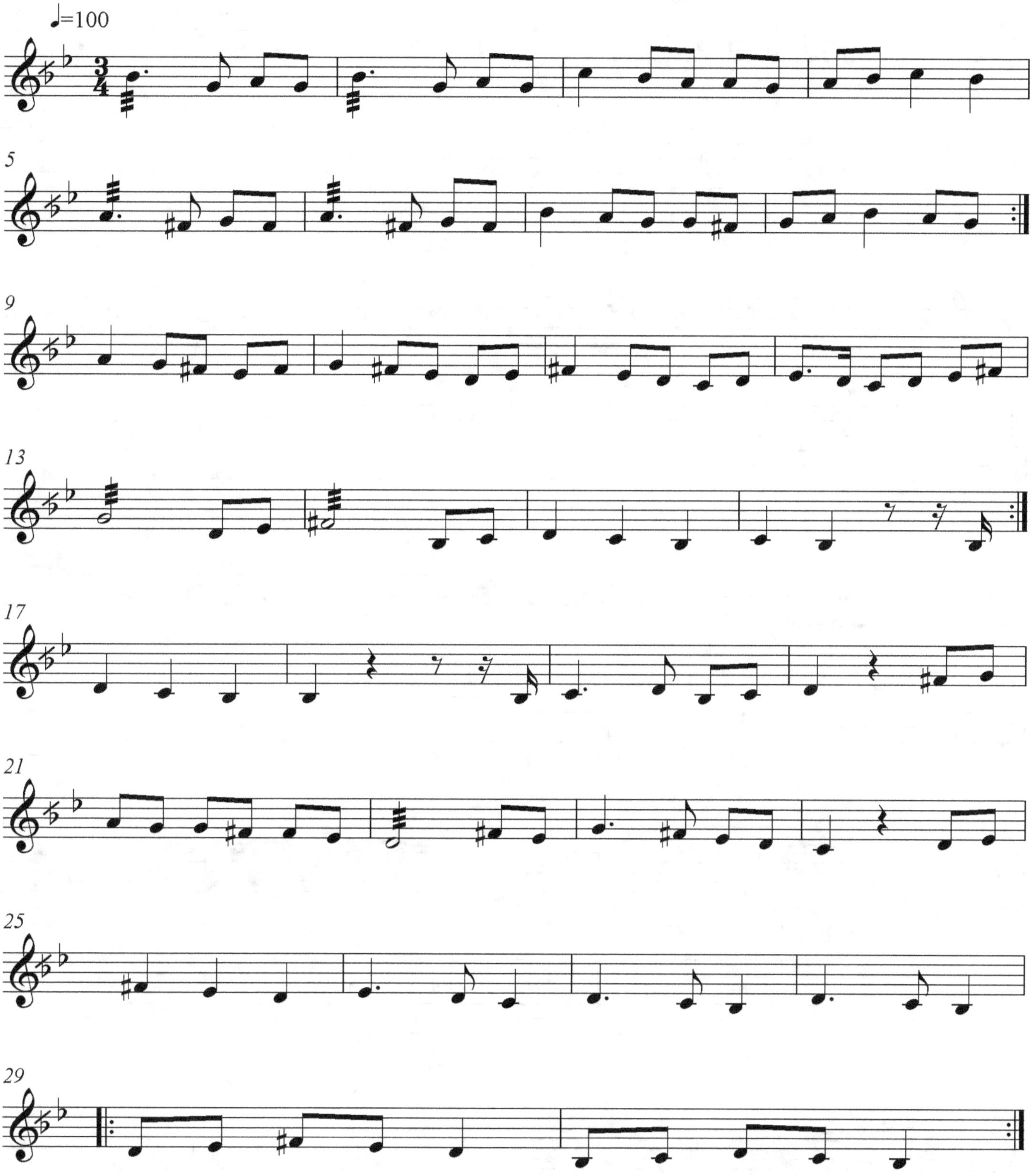

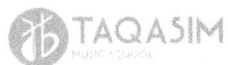

Daret al-Ayyam

The score below is part of a song made famous by *Umm Kulthoum*. It was written in *Maqam Huzam*.

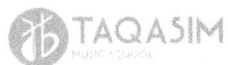

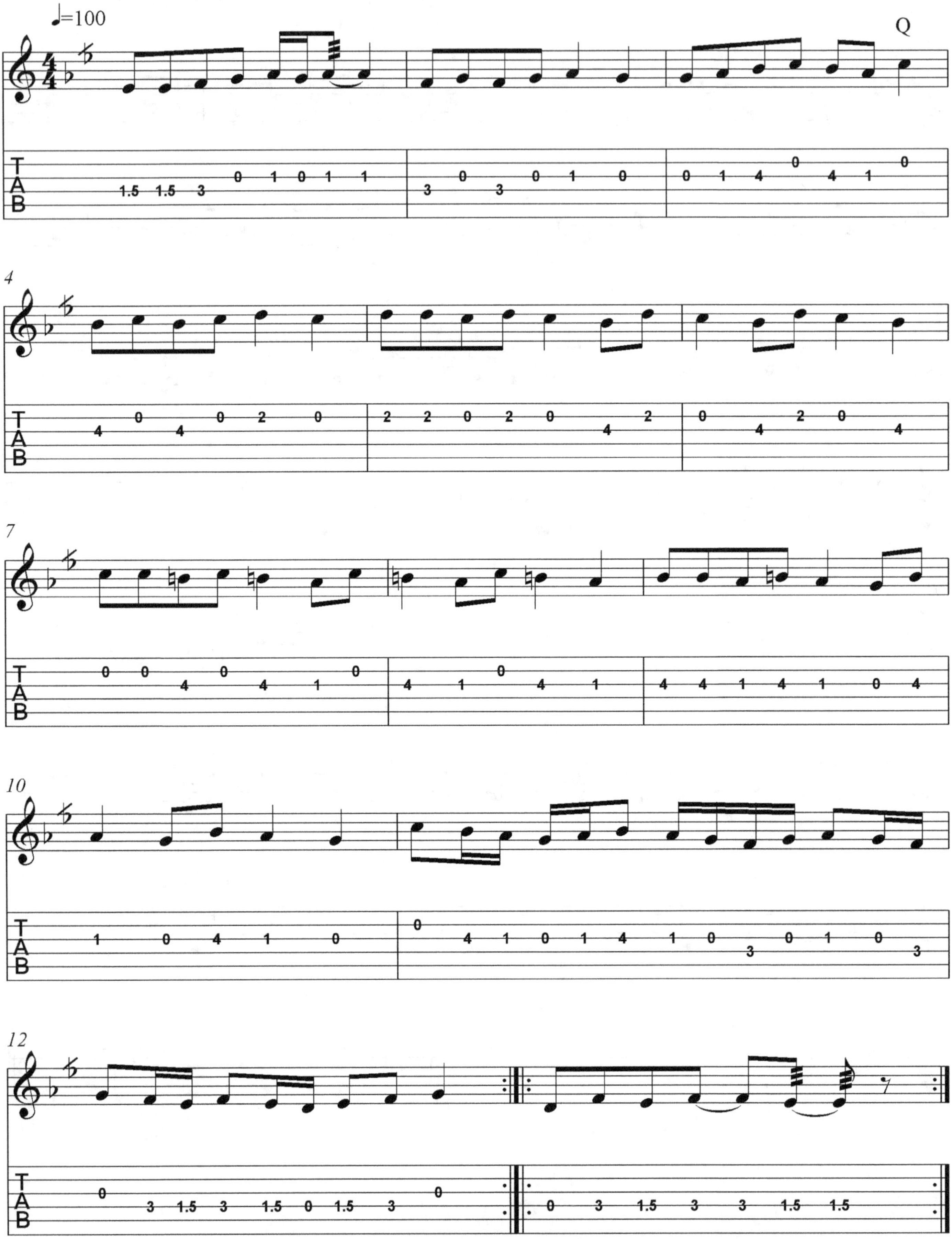

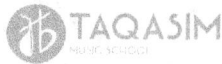

Repertoire Focus

The accumulation and application of musical knowledge while playing the Oud is important. Many pieces that have been covered in this book bring together a number of important skills in a single score. Those pieces are more important to master than others, as they encourage the performer to execute multiple skills at once. In turn, progressing his/her playing abilities.

The following is a list of pieces to focus on in this book:

1) *Longa Yurgo – Nahawand* Sol

2) *Etude Nagriz*

3) *Samaa'i Nagriz*

4) *Sulaf Bayat* Re

5) Samaa'i *Saba*

6) Blues Saba Sol

7) Al-Ward Gamil – *Huzam*

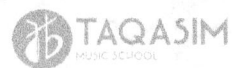

Extra Repertoire

In preparation for the Upper Advanced material, it is strongly advised that students practice the scales listed here. Scales that are written in 2 octaves using all 3 positions will help students prepare to begin playing masterpieces where all three positions are used.

One of the masterpieces that will be covered in the Upper Advanced book is *Caprice* by Jamil Bashir. It is written in *Nahawand* Do.

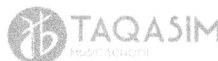

Maqam Nahawand – Played on One String

Nahawand Do – on the 5th string only

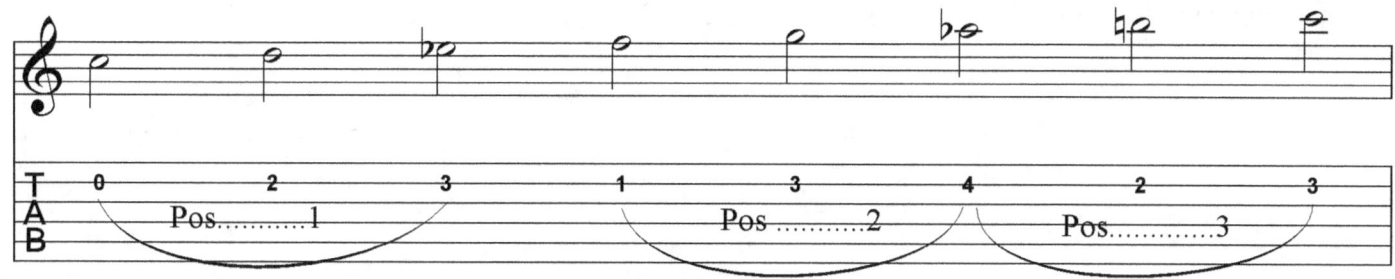

Nahawand Sol – 1st octave

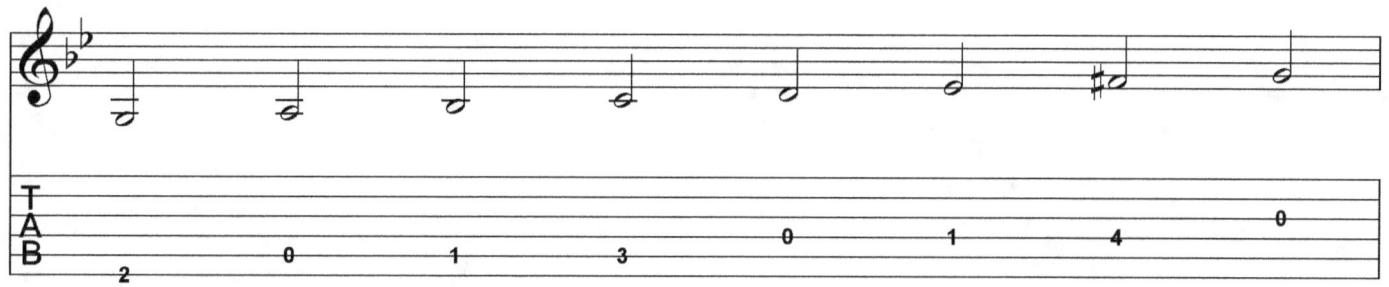

Nahawand Sol – on the 4th string only

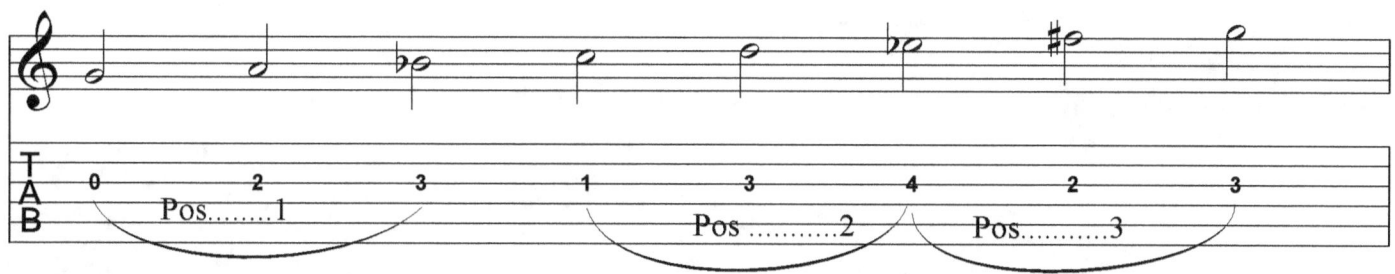

Nahawand Sol – on the 6th string only (3rd octave)

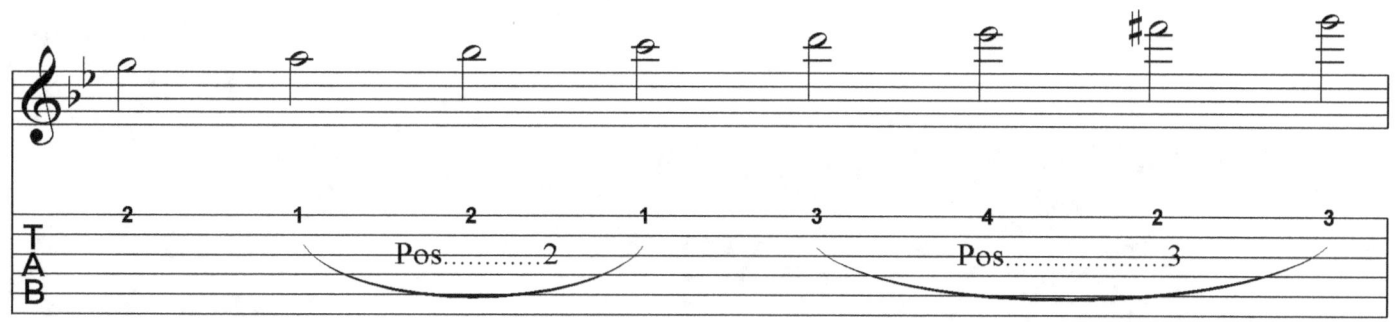

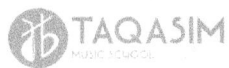

Caprice

Caprice is a form of composing derived from an Italian style of composition. It is usually extremely fast and uses a lot of triplets. Its aim is to show a high level of technique when playing a particular instrument. In Arabic music, a Caprice shows both a high level of technique as well as highlights the spirit/*rouhiyyah* of the maqam being used. Jamil Bashir's Caprice, is a good example of this.

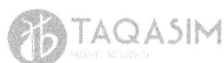

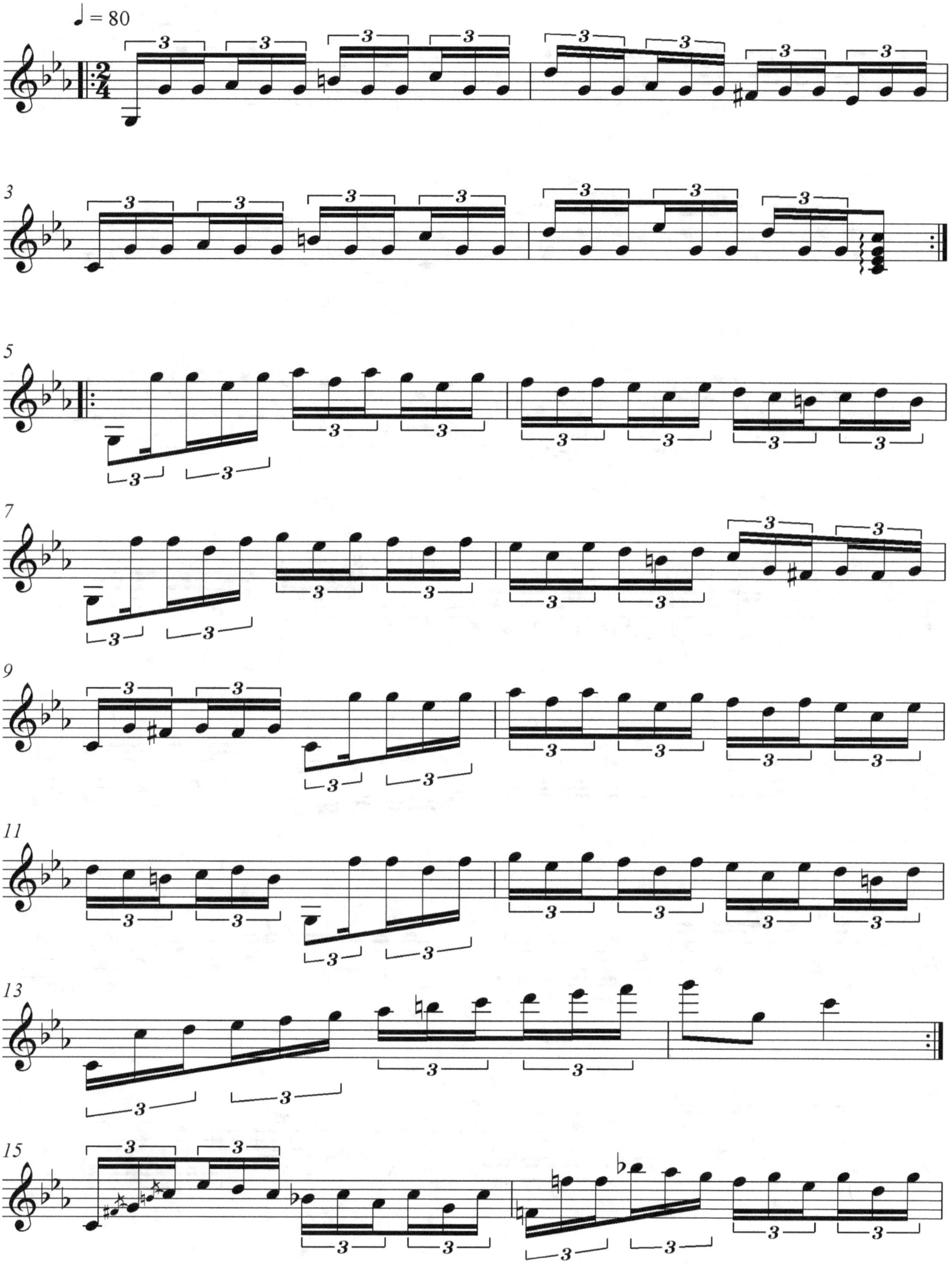

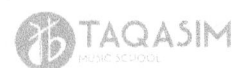

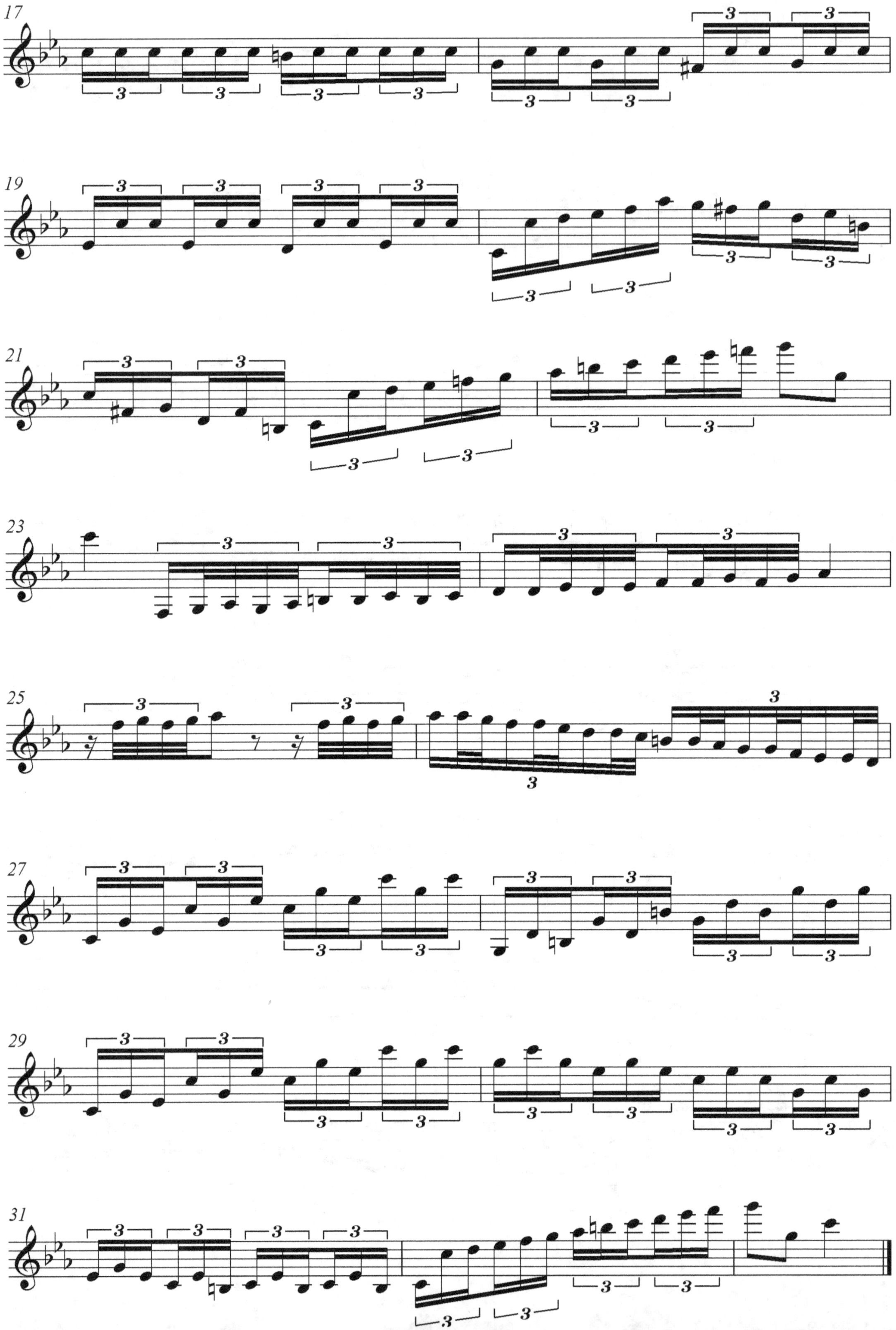

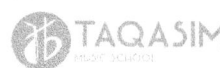

Maqamaat: Intervals and Tetrachords

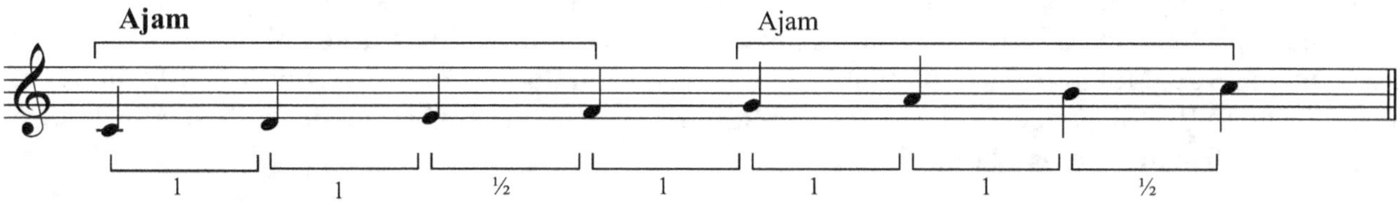

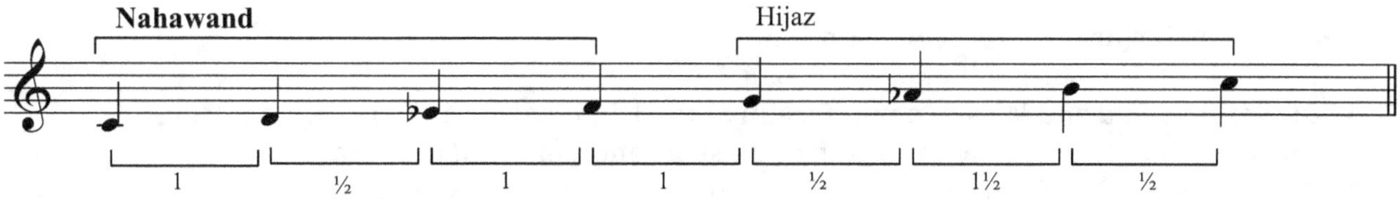

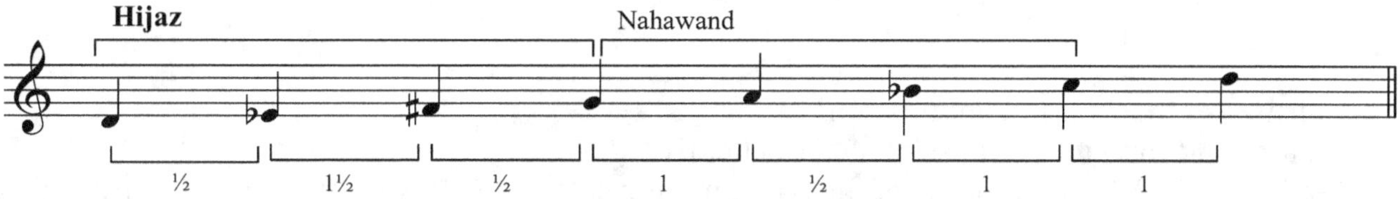

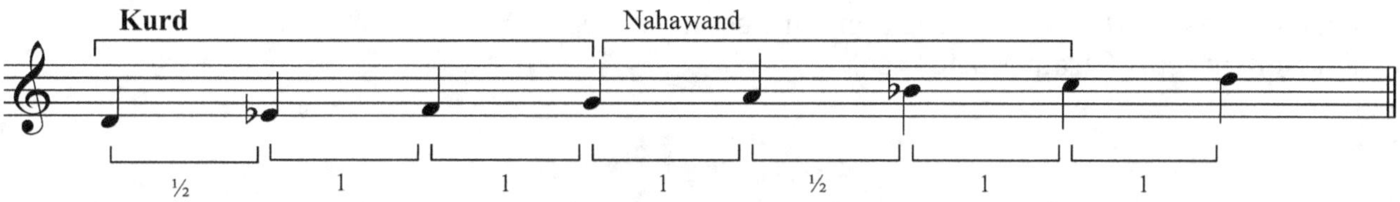

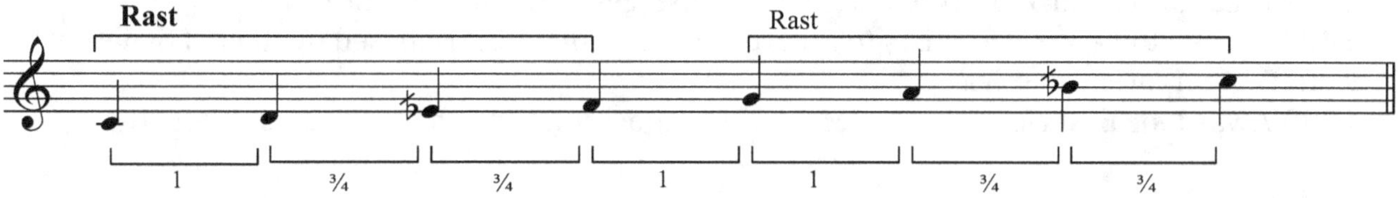

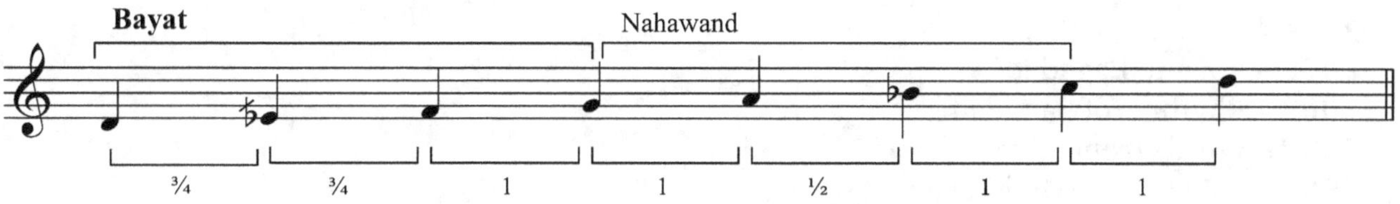

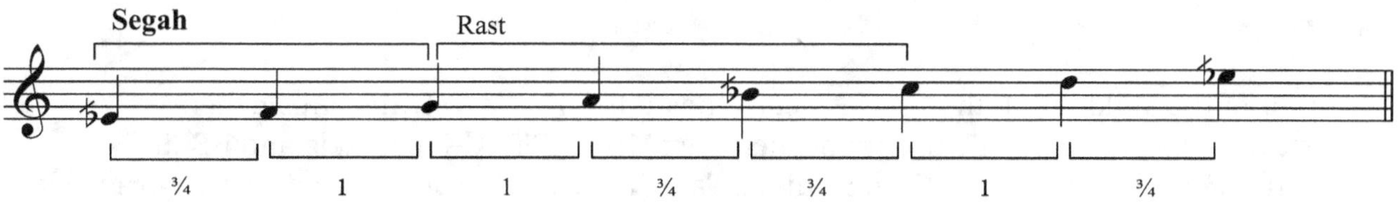

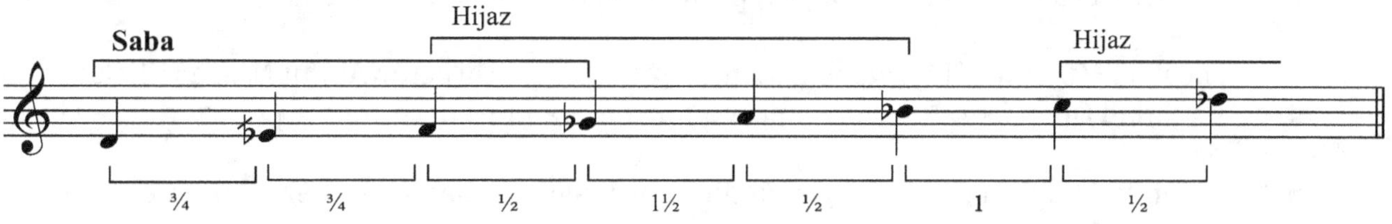

Ajam ... Ajam

Nahawand ... Hijaz

Hijaz ... Nahawand

Kurd ... Nahawand

Rast ... Rast

Bayat ... Nahawand

Segah ... Rast

Saba ... Hijaz ... Hijaz

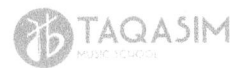

Ahmed Mukhtar

Born in Baghdad, Mukhtar has been playing the oud and Arabic percussions since 1979. In 1983, he began studying both the oud and percussion at the Institute of Fine Arts in Baghdad. A few years later, in 1990 he attended the High Institute of Music in Damascus where he continued his studies of the oud and Western percussions. In 1999, Mukhtar earned an MA from the London College of Music, and in 2003, he received a Masters Degree in Performance with a focus on Middle-Eastern and Arabic music from SOAS (the School of Oriental and African Studies), London.

Timeline

- **2003** MA in Performance – SOAS, London
- **1999** MA from the London College of Music
- **1990** Studied Oud and Western percussion at the High Institute of Music, Damascus
- **1985** Worked extensively with Arabic orchestras and performed on Iraqi TV
- **1983** Studied Oud and Percussion at the Institute of Fine Arts, Baghdad

Roles

- Chairman of the Taqasim Foundation
- Founder and Director of Taqasim Music School
- Member of the High Committee of the Babylon International Arts & Cultural Festival, Hilla, Iraq
- Producer and presenter of the "Solo Program"/"عزف منفرد", Al-Fayha, Iraqi TV
- Former Musical Director – Sleep Song project in France
- Former Director – Iraqi Music Week

Awards

- **2015** Award for Excellence in music composition
- **2009** Alhambra Award for Excellence under auspices of the Queen of Britain
- **2003** Chosen to be 1 of 16 artists to record original work a CD released by the UN benefiting victims of terrorism and war
- **1999** Award for Best Non-Western Musical Composition from the Musicians Union, UK

Discography

- **2015** – Babylonian Fingers
- **2005** – Road to Baghdad
- **2003** – Rhythms of Baghdad
- **1999** – Words from Eden
- **1997** – Tajwal (Live Oud Recital)

Other Work

- Author of the Mukhtar Method series: learn the oud, darbuka & Arabic music theory
- Musical compositions for TV programs including MBC, ART, Al-Mustakela and BBC5
- Theatre: Music composed for "The Soldier's Tale"; an Iraqi/Eurpoean rendition of Stravinsky's classical work directed by Andrew Bigley, performed at The Old Vic Theatre, London, UK in January 2006
- Musical Theatre: Music for "My Name is Jamal". by Algerian Director Abdul Nasser Khalaf
- Poetry: "Baghdad Open Sky" Music composed for the readings of dramatic poetry written by Saleh Al-Hamada
- Film: "Al-Baghdadi" a film by British/Iraqi director Mayham Riada; winner of The Gold Award at the International Filmmaker Festival

www.ingramcontent.com/pod-product-compliance
Lightning Source LLC
Chambersburg PA
CBHW081100180526
45170CB00005B/1831